CHRISTIAN
SOCIAL REFORMERS
OF THE NINETEENTH
CENTURY

CHRISTIAN
SOCIAL REFORMERS
OF THE NINETEENTH
CENTURY

by

JAMES ADDERLEY	CHARLES E. RAVEN
A. FENNER BROCKWAY	S. K. RUCK
A. J. CARLYLE	MARY SCHARLIEB
R. COUPLAND	CONSTANCE SMITH
HUGH MARTIN	WILLIAM TEMPLE
H. G. WOOD	

edited by
HUGH MARTIN

Essay Index Reprint Series

BOOKS FOR LIBRARIES PRESS
FREEPORT, NEW YORK

First Published 1927

Reprinted 1970

NOTE

It is perhaps unnecessary to remark that we are
aware that the title does not really cover Howard.
But in spirit if not in date he belongs to the
nineteenth century movement.   It seemed a pity
to spoil the title by over-anxious pedantry.

STANDARD BOOK NUMBER:

8369-1526-7

LIBRARY OF CONGRESS CATALOG CARD NUMBER:

70-107725

PRINTED IN THE UNITED STATES OF AMERICA

CONTENTS

v

ILLUSTRATIONS

INTRODUCTION: THE CHRISTIAN SOCIAL MOVEMENT IN THE NINETEENTH CENTURY

By WILLIAM TEMPLE, M.A., D.Litt.

THE
CHRISTIAN SOCIAL MOVEMENT IN
THE NINETEENTH CENTURY

THE history of the nineteenth century is, in one of its aspects, the history of the recovery of a forgotten part of Christian belief and practice. In the light of that recovery, many students in our own time have expended much labour in re-stating the teaching of Christian thinkers in earlier times, from the Early Fathers downwards. The weightiest and most important exposition hitherto is probably that of Mr R. H. Tawney, entitled *Religion and the Rise of Capitalism.* This and a host of other writings leave our generation without excuse if it fails to realise that as a plain matter of historic fact Christianity has, during the greater part of the whole period of its existence, deliberately set itself to exercise an influence on the political and social ordering of men's lives, and upon the economic relations between both individuals and classes.

It is important to make this quite plain, for otherwise the movements of the nineteenth century will be seen in an utterly false perspective. And indeed there are those who regard the whole enterprise of what is sometimes called Christian Socialism as the novel and paradoxical intrusion

3

of an alien element into the spiritual concerns of the Christian religion. It is nothing of the kind, though the long contraction of the scope of religious interest which reached its limit in the eighteenth century must have made it seem so when the tide first turned. No one, of course, who professes Christianity at all, denies that indirectly religion both should and does affect social questions, through the influence which it exerts upon individual character. Christians whose religion is a reality will be generous to the weak, sympathetic to the sick, kindly to the poor; and their individual action will alleviate the pressure of social evils; if there are enough real Christians, perhaps the burden of those evils will be altogether removed, except so far as they consist of " the thousand natural shocks that flesh is heir to." And no doubt it is on this side that the reawakening of conscience first shows itself. The accounts of Social Reformers in this book begin most properly with John Howard. It was no part of his business to deal with the question whether some who fell under the condemnation of the law could plead that their circumstances and training had given them little chance to become useful citizens. He was confronted with a vast mass of degradation, due to the casual neglect by public opinion of the condition of the prisons. No one planned the horrors which he exposed; they were neither part nor fruit of anything that could properly be called a punitive system; they were the result of a chaos which remained a chaos because no one felt any responsibility for bringing order into it.

John Howard illustrates a perfectly indispensable part of Christian duty. There can be no doubt at all about our duty to relieve suffering as far as we can, and to abolish casual suffering. And in so doing we shall to some small extent modify the social system which results in that suffering. And some would say that this is all that we can do as Christians. Such a view, in Höffding's famous metaphor, makes religion the ambulance corps of the army of progress, picking up and caring for the wounded and the weary, but will not allow it to be the pillar of cloud and fire which leads the army forward. It represents the laws of Political Economy as fixed independently of what men think or choose, like the laws of physics and chemistry. Within the system resulting from the operation of those laws we may be generous and sympathetic; to those who are in one way or another thrown out or broken by the system we may reach out helping hands, as Howard nobly called on the people of his generation to do to those in prison. But that is the limit. With the system itself Christianity must not meddle. If it does, it will do harm where it hopes to do good, for it will be defying unalterable laws; and it will damage itself for the discharge of its own mission, for it will secularise a message which should be purely spiritual. Such is the teaching given to us by many whom we cannot ignore.

But difficulties arise very quickly; for what constitutes a modification of the system? The second name in the series that follows must raise this question very acutely in our minds. Wilberforce was at first actuated by horrified sympathy for the slaves who were being shipped across the Atlantic for sale : but he was convinced that while the traffic continued at all such evils would attach to it. So he toiled and prayed for the abolition of the Slave Trade, and later for the abolition of slavery itself. He was impelled to this noble enterprise by his Christian faith. But there was no doubt that he was attacking the economic system of his own day. And no one now disputes that he was right to do so. So with the name that carries us over from the eighteenth century to the nineteenth we associate a profound modification of the social, industrial, and economic system carried through by Christian inspiration.

The same lesson is driven home by the name that follows. Shaftesbury, like Wilberforce, was stirred by sympathy for individuals. He had no theories about the Rights of Labour or any such abstractions. He was no democrat, and he actively disliked Trade Unions. But his conscience protested at the conditions under which men, women, and, above all, children were working in the factories. So he became the pioneer of factory legislation, deliberately invading the sphere of industrial and economic organisation in the name of humanity and at the dictation of Christian faith.

This brings us to the middle of the century, and already the principles implicit in the activities of Wilberforce and Shaftesbury are beginning to be worked out. In the sphere of religion itself the impulse to personal religion given by Wesley and

the Evangelical Revival had been supplemented
by that insistence on the essentially social or corporate nature of historic Christianity which was
a main contribution of the Oxford Movement ; so
religion itself was becoming less individualistic.
John Malcolm Ludlow, with F. D. Maurice,
Charles Kingsley and Thomas Hughes, represents
the next step forwards. Action had been taken,
and was being taken, on grounds of Christian
humanitarianism, which implied the claim that
Christian principles should regulate the economic
ordering of society. What then are the Christian
principles in question ? and what does their
application to actually existing conditions involve ?
The asking of those questions is the beginning of
Christian Socialism (which, of course, does not
historically represent any prejudging of the question, What should be the relation of Christianity
to the proposals of economic socialism in any of its
forms?). From this point onwards the predominant
question is not, How can we help such and such
sufferers ? but, What is the true Christian order
of society ?

This was a necessary advance ; but it involved
great dangers. First there was the danger that
the movement would become academic and lose
the impetus of strong human sympathy which had
carried it forward. Secondly, there was the danger
that it would become detached from the actual
facts and employ its energy in the fabrication
of purely ideal systems. Thirdly, there was the
danger, connected with both of the former, that
its adherents would talk a great deal of high-

sounding rhetoric, but would cease to do the job
that lay to hand in actually carrying the cause of
progress one stage further. The four names that
follow Ludlow's in this series are sufficient evidence
that these dangers can be avoided, but experience
is eloquent of the reality of those dangers, for to
some extent we have succumbed to them.

Students of our generation are apt to feel
irritation, or to assume a superior smile, when
they come across some of the considerations by
which Wilberforce sought to propagate content-
ment among the working classes, or read of Shaftesbury's fine Tory dislike of workmen's combina-
tions. But has our generation of generous phrases
and interminable conferences actually accomplished
in the social sphere anything at all comparable to
Abolition and the first Factory Acts ? We shall
do no good whatever if intellectual interest in the
problem comes to take a greater place in our
concern than personal sympathy for men and
women. Again, do we not find a vast amount of
energy consumed in describing society as it might
be, when there is no visible means of transforming
into that the society that actually is ? When I
read these constructions of the ideal state from
Plato's onward I always have two thoughts : one
is how odious life in that ideal state would be ;
the other is a recollection of the Irishman who,
being asked the way to Roscommon, replied, " If
I wanted to go to Roscommon, I wouldn't be
starting from here." Of course I shall be told
that we must fix our goal in order to determine
the direction in which we are to start. So Thomas

the Apostle said to our Lord, "We know not whither Thou goest; how know we the way?" The answer was, "I am the Way." And, indeed, Christianity provides no sketch of a social ideal; what it provides are principles by which we may act in any conceivable circumstances, and the power to do so if we will.

Once again, we find a vast amount of steam, which should be driving the engine, deliberately let off into the air in the form of high-falutin talk. There was never more discussion of large social themes among young men and women at the Universities than now. But the settlements are not full.

With the transference of attention from particular evils requiring remedy to the general problem of the better ordering of society there naturally arose organisations for the encouragement of study and the quickening of a sense of responsibility, such as the Christian Social Union with which the name of Henry Scott Holland is so closely associated. This was the Church of England Society; but before the nineteenth century closed every considerable Christian denomination had its formally constituted social service guild or union or committee. In the first decade of the twentieth century these began to draw together and to initiate joint enterprise. One product of that closer association was the great Conference on Politics, Economics and Citizenship held at Birmingham in 1924 and commonly known as C.O.P.E.C.

As a result of all that was done in the nineteenth

century it should be possible for us of the twentieth to see our task more clearly. What are we to say is the nature of the Church's concern with social problems ?

First, it is clear that a large part of the evils with which we are familiar would disappear if all men in purely personal dealings were considerate and courteous, as Christians ought to be.

Secondly, it is also clear that if we loved our neighbours as ourselves we should both be active in the philanthropic enterprises which care for those who are not strong enough for the stress of life or which try to give better opportunities of personal development than many could otherwise enjoy ; and we should also be eager in such matters as hastening the supply of houses for the poorer classes, for we should be as greatly distressed at our neighbour's child having to grow up in a slum as at our own children, or brothers and sisters, suffering that fate.

So far there is no dispute ; and if all Christians went so far a great deal would be accomplished. But if Shaftesbury was justified in the action which he took (and no one now doubts that he was), or still more if Ludlow was justified, there is a further step to be taken. We may put it in this way.

Professor Marshall, the great " orthodox " political economist of the last generation, laid it down that the greatest influence in the formation of character, next to religion, is that of the economic system under which men live. Formation of character is the Church's first concern ; it will then rightly be eager that the economic system shall be such as to co-operate with it rather than resist it in that fundamental responsibility.

The Church, out of loyalty to its own first duty, is therefore bound to criticise the social and industrial order to see how far its influence tends to the formation of a Christian type of character, and what modifications in it are both possible and desirable with that object in view.

" All very well," says the objector ; " but however much Christianity might wish to modify the existing order, the thing is impossible. The laws of political economy are fixed like the laws of nature, and the economic system of any moment is the product of their operation hitherto. What you have to do is to observe them and shape your conduct with a view to any desired result in the light of them. But if you try to frame a system other than these laws produce, it will collapse, and you will merely have invited disaster."

Now there are certain laws or principles of which this is true, but they are not very many, and on investigation they all turn out to be neither more nor less than applied arithmetic. They are such principles as these : You cannot distribute what has not been produced ; you cannot permanently run any business at a loss. These platitudes are indeed sometimes ignored. But the laws usually intended by those who compare economic laws to laws of nature are something far more elaborate than these. The chief one is the law of supply and demand, which tells us that if supply exceeds demand, prices must fall, whereas if demand exceeds supply, prices must rise; because price is fixed at the point which equalises supply and demand. Thus, if A wishes to buy X from B, and B asks for £100 while A offers £1, no transaction takes place. If next day B will accept £90 while A offers £10, there is still no transaction. But if they continue to move at the same pace, there will come a time when each will name £50, 10s. as the price, and a purchase will be effected.

But it is perfectly clear that we are here in the region of the human will. The law of supply and demand only works so long as both parties to the transaction desire to give as little as they need and to gain as much as they can. That is so predominant a temper in commerce that a law based upon it has a very wide application. But that law is neither necessary nor universal. And if people's wills were modified, the law would be modified.[1]

But our task as Christians is not to construct an ideal state in thought or imagination and then transform the actual into some resemblance to that ideal: our task is to apply certain principles with ever greater thoroughness to the world in which we live. Those principles are, or at any rate include, these four: the Sacredness of Personality; the Fact of Membership or Fellowship; the Duty of Service; the Power of Self-sacrifice.

Christians will differ about the wisdom or expediency of particular proposals that may be

[1] For a further development of this point see Chap. VI. in my book, *Personal Religion and the Life of Fellowship* (Longmans).

made ; and for this reason the Church must not be committed to any party or programme, and Christians who advocate programmes must be careful to avoid the suggestion that their proposal is one which all Christians ought to support. But there is no room for reasonable doubt about the responsibility of Christians to care for these things and to press forward the application to our actual social order of the social principles inherent in the Gospel.

Painting by
M. Brown

National Portrait
Gallery

JOHN HOWARD

JOHN HOWARD (1726–90)
By S. KENNETH RUCK, B.A.

JOHN HOWARD

I. The Prisons

Two centuries ago, when Howard was born, the general attitude towards the criminal was one of complacent brutality. This was due to no one single cause. Wrong-headed, unchristian, even positively wicked theory, combined with corrupt practice to produce it ; it was fostered by official neglect and public apathy.

Any theory of the treatment of criminals which reflects Christianity must regard, or even must take as a guiding principle, the injunction to do good to them that despitefully use you ; therefore reformation is essential. Not only the New Testament, but even the Old, insists on the incompetence of men to assess punishment for moral wrongs ; therefore retribution is impossible. Yet in the penal methods of the eighteenth century the idea of reform, which had never had more than a sickly and spasmodic existence, was wholly dead, and the ideas of retribution and its grisly first cousin deterrence were all-powerful.

Whatever the theory, however, the practice did not correspond. In most cases it was worse ; where it was better, as, for instance, in the facilities allowed a prisoner for seeing his friends and family, the fact was due to accident and not design.

For the theory was (so far as a theory existed among a mass of ill-considered and unrelated statutes) that punishment must be frightful, and that the most frightful thing to do with a man was to take his life, or else tear him from his home and kindred and cast him into the wilderness on the other side of the world. The practice always cast him into prison. The other things might or might not follow—even the sluggish public conscience of that day would not tolerate the death sentence for the multitude of offences for which it was legal, and the transport part of the transportation was always a difficulty.

Thus the prisons became the central feature of the penal methods of the day and some of the horrors which they contained and the miseries they inflicted may be gathered by quotations given later in this paper. Yet imprisonment was *not* punitive in intention. Prisons were, so to speak, remand homes, where felons were kept pending their trial, their transportation or their execution, and debtors pending the payment of their debts. Nor were they punitive in effect on the successful felon or fraudulent debtor who had money at his command, since every sort of concession could be bought from a gaoler who not only was not paid for his office but had probably himself paid for it and paid dearly.[1]

On the other hand, an honest debtor, the victim of imprudence or misfortune, suffered the bitterest extremities in his confinement, being starved, and

---

[1] At the beginning of the century the lease of the wardenship of the Fleet prison was bought by a notorious scoundrel named Bambridge for £5000.

sometimes literally rotted, because his very plight made it impossible for him to meet those extortions which were the price of the barest comfort.

Concerning the Bridewells, the only institutions which *were* reformative and punitive in intention, since they had been designed for the redemption of rogues, vagabonds and idle apprentices, it is sufficient to quote the opinion of Fielding that they were " no other than Schools of Vice, Seminaries of Idleness and common shores of Nastiness and Disease," distinguishable only from the prisons by the greater probability of total starvation for their wretched denizens, since they had no allowance of food from the county rate.

The evils which were thus sown by a cruel theory and insensate practice were plentifully nourished by official neglect and public apathy. There was no central authority to check abuses, while the sheriffs and county magistrates who were responsible for the condition of their gaols were too terrified of the fever which resulted from their own unfaithfulness to inspect more than the outside of the buildings.

That there was no public opinion able to remedy such a state of things was largely because the paucity of communications did not allow expression to be given to the accumulated weight of horrors that existed, and even if it had been given, an uneducated populace would hardly have been able to grasp its import. Yet there were many who could read and many who could hardly have failed to remember that Christ regarded them not as his friends who would not visit him when sick and in prison. Thus not all the blame could be fastened on the theorists and the statesmen, the gaolers and the magistrates.

It is not to be thought or expected, however, that no single individual ever sought to alleviate some of the worst distress and to reform some of the grosser abuses. Attempts were made, committees formed and even Bills passed, only to fall into almost immediate oblivion, in company with the majority of reformative legislation in the century.

Something more was needed than the philanthropist who would make his plea and then be silent, or see an Act on the Statute Book and then rest satisfied. Indeed, philanthropy was not enough; some deeper and more compelling motive was required to fit a man to brave the dangers, face the hardships and display the persistence necessary to remedy the state of prisons.

The motive existed in Christianity; the man in whom it found expression was John Howard.

II. HOWARD

When he was forty-five years old, Howard wrote these words in his Journal :—

" Oh, compassionate and divine Redeemer, save me from the dreadful Guilt and power of Sin and accept of my solemn free and I trust unreserved surrender of my Soul, my Spirit, my dear Child, all I am and have, into Thy hands ! unworthy of Thy acceptance ! . . .

" Thus, oh my Lord and my God, is humbly bold even a *worm* to covenant with Thee ! do Thou

ratify and confirm it and make me the everlasting
monument of Thy unbounded Mercy. Amen.
Amen. Amen.

"Hoping my heart deceives me not and trusting
in His Mercy . . . with fear and trembling I sign
my unworthy Name. JOHN HOWARD."
NAPLES, 27th *May* 1770.

N.B.—This Solemn Covenant renewed at
Moscow.
27th *September* 1789.

When this covenant was made, although he was
well advanced into middle age, there was little
in Howard's present condition or past history to
suggest that he was the reformer the country needed.

The present showed him to be a country gentleman, of considerable fortune but inconspicuous
address, travelling Europe in search of health, for,
so far from being robust, he was even something of
a valetudinarian.

And his past was almost ludicrously unheroic.
His father, a prosperous city upholsterer, after
giving him an indifferent education—at least so far
as scholarship was concerned—had apprenticed him
to a grocer. His death shortly afterwards left
Howard comparatively wealthy, and at the age of
twenty-five, as a mark of independence, he married
—a widow of fifty-two who had been his landlady.
The marriage, which Howard entered upon from a
sense of gratitude in spite of the lady's objections,
nevertheless proved a quietly happy one, and on his
wife's death, after three years, Howard sought con-
solation in travel. It was then there occurred the

solitary event of his earlier years which seems to
show a direct connection with his life's work ; the
boat on which he left England was captured by a
French privateer, and, as a result, Howard himself
experienced the miseries of a dungeon. He was not
long detained, being released on parole, but on
arrival in England at once busied himself to secure
the release of his fellow sufferers. That done, he
returned once again to his country estate at Cardington, near Bedford. Here, three years later, he
married a second time. This second marriage was
of a very different nature from the first, though
even here the wooing must have been sober and
practical, for Howard stipulated that, in any post-
marital dispute that might arise, his opinion was to
prevail ! His second wife was, however, of an age
with himself, similar in tastes and in temperament
and as much in love with him as he with her. As a
result they spent seven years of almost perfect
happiness together, during which Cardington was
converted from one of the most miserable to one of
the most prosperous villages in the country. The
model cottages Howard built for his tenants are
standing to this day and form one of the pleasantest
features of a very pleasant village.

But the greater the happiness, the greater the
debt incurred to sorrow, and Howard paid dearly
when, in 1765, shortly after giving birth to a son, his
wife died. Howard saw his child through its years
of infancy, then, his health showing signs of failing,
sought refuge in travel once more, and it was while
he was on this, his fourth, continental journey, that
he entered into the Covenant detailed above.

On his return to England, Howard, by exerting himself to promote the prosperity of his tenants, continued in the widest sphere of service which had as yet opened itself to him, until in 1773 chance or circumstance or Providence—Howard knew which, if we pretend to doubt—decreed his election to the office of Sheriff of the County. This was generally regarded as a merely formal honour, like a modern honorary degree, and was held to involve about the same responsibilities, *i.e.*, the wearing of gorgeous raiment at certain public functions.

The result Howard tells us himself.

"The distress of prisoners," he says at the beginning of his great book, *The State of the Prisons*, ". . . came more immediately under my notice when I was Sheriff of the county of Bedford, and the circumstances which excited me to activity in their behalf was the seeing, some—who by the verdict of Juries were declared *not guilty* ; some—on whom the Grand Jury did not find such an appearance of guilt as subjected them to trial ; and some—whose prosecutors did not appear against them ; after having been confined for months, dragged back to gaol and locked up again till they should pay *sundry fees* to the gaoler, the clerk of assize, etc.

"In order to redress this hardship, I applied to the justices of the county for a salary to the gaoler in lieu of his fees. The bench were properly affected with the grievance and willing to grant the relief desired : but they wanted a precedent for charging the county with the expense. I therefore rode into several neighbouring counties in search of one ; but I soon learned that the same injustice was practised in them; and, looking into the prisons, I beheld scenes of calamity, which I grew daily more and more anxious to alleviate.

" . . . I was called to the first part of my task by my office of Sheriff. To the pursuit of it I was prompted by the sorrows of the sufferers and love to my country. The work grew upon me insensibly. I could not enjoy my ease and leisure in neglect of an opportunity offered me by Providence of attempting the relief of the miserable."

Howard knew now the task that lay before him. He had offered his life to whatsoever service God should demand of him and the call had come. Henceforth he sacrificed—literally made sacred— his leisure, his wealth, his comfort, everything he had and everything he was, to the cause he had taken up.

Some idea of the extent of his exertions can be gathered from a note in one of his memorandum books. It must be remembered first that these were the days of slow coaches, whose memory only survives as a derision, and, secondly, that the note covers only about two-thirds of the period of his prison journeys, which he continued until he died in Russia in 1790.

"AN ACCOUNT OF THE NUMBER OF MILES TRAVELLED ON THE REFORM OF PRISONS

Journeys.		Miles.
In Great Britain and Ireland. . 1773–6		10,318
First Foreign Journey . . . 1775		1,400
Second ditto 1776		1,700
Third ditto. 1778		4,636
	Carry forward	18,054

Journeys.				*Miles.*
		Brought forward		18,054
In Great Britain and Ireland.	.	.	1779	6,490
Fourth Foreign Journey	.	.	1781	4,465
In Great Britain and Ireland.	.	.	1782	8,165
Fifth Foreign Journey .	.	.	1783	3,304
To Ireland .	.	.	..	715
To Worcester	.	.	..	238
To Hertford, Chelmsford, and Warrington	.	.	..	602
		Total	.	42,033

To God alone be all praise! I do not regret
the Loss of many Conveniences of Life, but bless
God who inclined my mind to such a Scheme."

III. Howard and the Prisons—Fact

I

Howard's undertaking was unusual enough to
gain a swift fame. It happened that at about the
time when he began his inspection of the prisons,
one of those periodic Bills for the amelioration of
some unusually glaring defect was before the House.
Howard was called upon to give evidence, and the
fact of his having first-hand knowledge, combined
with an ability to present it forcibly, so astounded
his hearers that he was summoned to the bar of the
House to receive the thanks of Parliament, an almost
unprecedented honour for a mere civilian. It was
the one mark of honour, too, that Howard, a
convinced democrat, was likely to value, and he

treasured the memory of it when proposals to erect a statue to him roused in him an almost passionate resentment.

The Bill, which was for the abolition of Gaolers' fees and the better attention of the sick, was passed, as other Bills had been passed before. Howard, at his own expense, had copies of it printed for hanging in every gaol, with the result that its memory at least was prolonged so long as the paper lasted. Meanwhile he proceeded with his investigations, and by 1775, having in the meantime providentially escaped election to Parliament himself, had completed them sufficiently to consider bringing them to the public notice.

At this point, however, as he characteristically expresses it, " conjecturing that something useful to my purpose might be collected abroad, I laid aside my papers and travelled into France, Flanders, Holland and Germany." Even then he was not satisfied that his knowledge was sufficiently extensive or accurate for committal to print, but set out on another inspection of English gaols to correct any errors into which he might hitherto have fallen, and followed that up by a second continental tour. Then at last he felt he was himself sufficiently acquainted with the facts to perform his duty of enlightening others. At the same time, being fully conscious of the defects of his education, he was not willing to let his case suffer from the lack of an adequate presentation, and accordingly enlisted the aid of a learned friend to polish his phrases. If further proof were needed to show that Howard felt himself to be engaged in a sacred mission in publishing his book, it may be found in the account which Brown, his first and best biographer, gives of his daily habit when at Warrington, where the printing was being done.

" So indefatigable was he in his attention to the business which had fixed his temporary abode there, that during a very severe winter he was always called up by two in the morning, though he did not retire to rest until ten, and sometimes half after ten, at night. His reason for his early rising was that he found the morning the stillest part of the day, and that in which he was least disturbed in his work of revising the sheets as they came from the press."

At the beginning of April the printing was finished, and Howard, who had taken the utmost care to see that the form of the book should be worthy of its matter, now devoted equal pains to see that its message gained the widest possible appeal, not only by selling it at a price at which " had every copy been sold, he would still have presented the public with all the plates, and a great part of the printing," but also by giving copies of it wherever a knowledge of its contents was likely to bring about an improvement of the conditions it exposed.

II

This first edition of *The State of the Prisons* consisted of five sections with the following titles :— " A General View of Distress in the Prisons," " Bad Customs in Prisons," " Proposed Improvements in the Structure and Management of Prisons," " An

c

Account of Foreign Prisons," and " A Particular Account of English Prisons."

A few quotations from what is and will remain a classic work will serve better than any attempt at a description of it. It should be remembered in reading, however, that Howard had a horror of rhetoric as he had of exaggeration, and that a little imagination is needed to fill out the picture the bare words suggest.

From Sections I, II, and III.

Food.—" There are several bridewells in which prisoners have no allowance of food at all."

" Many criminals are half starved : such of them as at their commitment were in health come out almost famished, scarce able to move, and for weeks incapable of any labour."

Water.—" Many prisons have no water."

Bedding.—" In many gaols, and in most bridewells, there is no allowance of bedding or straw for prisoners to sleep on. . . . Some lie upon rags, others upon the bare floor."

Use of Irons.—" Loading prisoners with *heavy irons* which make their walking, and even lying down to sleep, difficult and painful, is another custom which I cannot but condemn. Even the women do not escape this severity.

" The practice must be mere tyranny : unless it proceeds from avarice, which I rather suspect ; because county gaolers do sometimes indulge their prisoners with what they call ' the choice of irons ' if they will pay for it."

Health.—" Certain it is that many of those who

survive their long confinement are by it rendered incapable of working. Some of them by scorbutic distempers, others by their toes mortified and quite rotted from their feet, many instances of which I have seen."

" My clothes were in my first journies so offensive that in a post chaise I could not bear the windows drawn up. . . . The leaves of my memorandum book were often so tainted that I could not use it till after spreading it an hour or two before the fire, and even my antidote, a vial of vinegar, has, after using it in a few prisons, become intolerably disagreeable. I did not wonder that in those journies many gaolers made excuses ; and did not go with me into the felons' wards."

" I have asked some keepers, since the late Act for preserving the health of prisoners, why no care is taken of their sick ; and have been answered that the magistrates tell them the *Act does not extend to bridewells.*"

The Insane.—" In some few gaols are confined Idiots and Lunatics. Where these are not kept separate, they distract and terrify other prisoners."

Moral Taint.—" I have now to complain of what is pernicious to their *morals* ; and that is, the confining of all sorts of prisoners together : debtors and felons, men and women, the young beginner and the old offender : and with all these, in some counties, such as are guilty of misdemeanours only ; who should have been committed to bridewell to be corrected ; but for want of food and the means of procuring it are in pity sent to such county gaols as afford these offenders prison allowance."

After the horrors revealed in the first and second section, the suggestions for improvements contained in the third seem so obvious that it is difficult to remember how revolutionary they were. Adequate supplies of food, water (for washing as well as drinking purposes), bedding and air ; separate confinement by night ; segregation of men and women, debtors and felons, old and young offenders ; proper hospital accommodation ; workshops ; regular inspection ; abolition of gaol fees and the " tap,"[1] and the substitution of a salary to the gaoler ; all are embodied in this brief but comprehensive scheme of prison reform, the first of any note to gain currency in this country.[2] It can safely be said that, wherever prison practice of to-day represents an improvement on the practice of that time, the improvement was forecasted by Howard. One can even find the germ of the idea of House masters in Borstal Institutions.

The section on the foreign prisons is interesting chiefly as showing how far superior prison conditions were in some countries, notably Holland, Switzerland and Belgium, to those in England.

The fifth section, by far the largest in the book, contains detailed information about every prison and bridewell in the country. In the case of each

[1] The sale of liquor was the gaoler's chief source of income ; the more he sold the greater his profits. Hence much of the moral degradation of the prisons.

[2] Some of Howard's reforms still remain to be achieved. Even in his own country this segregation of old and young offenders is not yet complete, while in many places abroad there is no separation at night, and the supply of fresh air and the hospital accommodation often leave much to be desired.

prison a statistical summary—giving the names and salaries of gaoler, [the word " none " generally appears] Chaplain and Surgeon ; fees and garnish[1] payable by and allowance of bread due to debtors and felons respectively ; type of licence (whether for beer only or for beer and wine), and number of prisoners, is followed by a paragraph giving details of the situation, accommodation and general condition of the building.

Some of these paragraphs suggest unimaginable horrors, such as this, on Knaresboro' Prison :—

" Earth floor: no fire : very offensive; a common sewer from the town running through it uncovered. I was informed that an officer, confined here some years since, took in with him a dog to defend him from vermin ; but the dog was soon destroyed and the prisoner's face much disfigured by them."

Or this, on the town gaol at Plymouth :—

" Three rooms for felons, etc., and two rooms over them for debtors. One of the former, the *clink*, 15 feet by 8 feet 3 inches and about 5½ feet high, with a wicket in the door 7 inches by 5 to admit light and air. To this, as I was informed, three men, who were confined near two months under sentence for transportation, came by turns for breath."

---

[1] In nearly all gaols, the latest arrival was required to produce a certain sum to be spent at the tap " for the good of the house." Failure to comply usually involved " running the gauntlet."

III

With the publication of *The State of Prisons*, Howard had made the greatest single contribution towards the reform of the prisons that lay in his power. He was now an elderly man and might reasonably have gone into a comfortable retirement in the picturesque and comfortable house at Cardington. But he would not have been Howard had he done so. For he must have known that there was none beside himself who would or could carry on the inspection of the gaols which he had so vehemently urged, no one who could relieve the distress of individual prisoners as he had done.

Accordingly, the greater part of his remaining years were devoted to a continuance of the task he had begun. Besides making investigations on the Continent, he visited every English prison afresh not only once, but twice, thrice, and even in some cases six times and carefully noted the improvements or deteriorations in successive editions of his book. The Hulks—disused battleships rigged up to accommodate the overflowing transportees—were also inspected, and in this connection Howard was once more called upon to give his evidence to the House of Commons. The conditions he found in the Hulks were even more shocking than in the bridewells and county gaols, and, as a result of his unhesitating condemnation, certain improvements were effected. Other Bills were passed for the improvement of prison conditions, most of them meeting the usual fate of their kind, though one, for erecting a new type of prison on the model of the

Maison de Force at Ghent,[1] which had won Howard's high praise, seemed likely to have a better fate. This had the full weight of Howard's influence and exertions behind it as well as those of his friends, but the scheme was eventually wrecked owing to disputes as to the site which the prison should occupy.

In 1785, feeling that, for the moment at any rate, he had done all that lay in his power in connection with the prisons, he embarked upon a new enterprise. This was an enquiry into the cause and treatment of the plague, the frightful effects of which he had witnessed in his earlier journeys.

This enquiry carried him through France and Italy to Malta, Asia Minor and Turkey, and on his return journey he purposely risked infection in order that he might himself undergo the regulation forty days of quarantine in Venice. It is difficult in these days of enlightened medical science to conceive the horrors and dangers to which he thus voluntarily exposed himself. Howard, however, shrank from doing nothing which he thought could in any way contribute to human happiness.

On his return to England he published the result of his investigations, made one final tour of inspection of the English prisons, then set off once more in search of further information concerning the lazarettos. This proved to be his last journey. At Cherson, near the borders of the Black Sea, he was

---

[1] The *Maison de Force* is still in use. The citizens of Ghent regard it with pride as a tribute to their own enlightenment; others with sorrow as a cenotaph to the spirit of reform.

entreated to visit and prescribe for the daughter of one of the neighbouring families who had fallen a victim to a prevailing infectious fever. As a result of his treatment, her condition improved, but some days later a further urgent message, requesting Howard's presence, again was sent. The delivery of this message was somehow delayed and, on receiving it, Howard felt his attendance must be immediate. No conveyance being available, he had to set off at once on the back of the first mount that offered, a dray horse, though the night was wild and tempestuous. On his arrival, drenched and benumbed from his protracted journey, he found his patient near her death. He must then have himself contracted the fever, and a day or two later, the symptoms manifesting themselves, he knew at once that his own death was approaching. He met it with the quiet faith which had marked his life, and his last request to a friend was in these words : " Let me beg of you, as you value your old friend, not to suffer any pomp to be used at my funeral ; . . . but lay me quietly in the earth, place a sundial over my grave, and let me be forgotten."

Howard's wishes were not respected. A marble tomb was erected over his grave in place of a sundial, but for once a not unworthy inscription was chosen.

JOHN HOWARD

WHOEVER THOU ART, THOU STANDEST AT

THE TOMB OF THY FRIEND

1790

IV. HOWARD AND THE PRISONS—CAUSE

No one can read Howard's life and remain in any doubt as to the cause of his undertaking his mission. He believed God had called him to it. But assuming that Howard was right, and that Christ summoned His disciples then and now as surely as He did on the borders of Galilee, why should Howard have been chosen for the task, a middle-aged, ailing, ex-grocer's apprentice ?

First, he was brave, and in one who had to visit pestilence-ridden dungeons that even doctors shrank from, courage was a first necessity. Such courage Howard showed almost every day of his life, and the one occasion upon which a rather more spectacular variety was needed, Howard met as he might have been expected to meet it. A vessel upon which he was travelling in the Mediterranean was surprised by a Tunisian privateer and was in danger of capture when Howard himself fired the solitary cannon his boat possessed, loaded to the muzzle with old nails, spikes, etc., into the enemy crew. As a result the enemy sheered off, and Howard, with the rest of his companions, escaped being butchered or sold into slavery, or more probably blown up, since Howard's captain, having decided that this was a more desirable fate than falling into the hands of the enemy, had made preparations accordingly.

Physical courage, however, is comparatively common ; moral courage, of the type that Howard possessed, rare indeed. Every day of his life the comfort so well within his reach beckoned him from the hardships and dangers he had undertaken, and as he progressed along the narrow path he had chosen, the temptations that faced him did not lessen ; his growing fame led kings and princes all over Europe to flatter and to seek to entertain. Howard's method was the same with all ; if he felt their interest could further his work he agreed to see them, and then told them all the most unpalatable facts he knew about their prison administration. Otherwise he sent a message to say he was too busy.

Howard was also thorough. He was never content with a statement on hearsay when he could confirm it with a personal investigation and did not care in the least what time and trouble he spent in the collection of his facts. In this connection a pregnant footnote to his *Remarks on the Gaol Fever* may be quoted.

" It may not be improper here to put persons on their guard against an artifice not infrequently practised by gaolers in order to prevent a proper examination of their prisons. When a gentleman, particularly a magistrate, has come with an intention to visit the gaol, the keeper has pretended the utmost willingness to accompany him, but at the same time has artfully dropped a hint that he fears there may be some danger in it, as he is apprehensive that *the fever* has made its appearance among them. The visitor, alarmed, returns thanks for the kind caution, and instantly leaves the house. On such occasions I have always the more insisted on the necessity of a close inspection ; and have generally found the prison very dirty, indeed, and out of order, but no *fever*."

Howard was sane. His zeal never carried him into the fanaticism or sentimentality that so often ruins a good cause ; his proposals were always sober and practical. In this respect his business apprenticeship at the grocer's store, no doubt, served him in good stead. Even his charities were guided by solid good sense. The postillions in his day were evidently as extortionate and ungracious as some taximen in ours. Howard had his own method of dealing with them. At the end of a journey, if he had reason to be dissatisfied with the conduct of his driver, he would cause him to be summoned to his presence in company with a needy widow of the village. He would then pay the postillion his bare legal fare, but in order to show that it was not meanness which actuated him, would hand over to the widow, in the presence of the disgusted driver, the generous extras that would have been his had he earned them.

Howard loved his fellow-men. One feels that a large part of the appeal of his prison mission was the scope it gave him for relieving the distresses of those most in need of comfort. Though there is little evidence in proof, for Howard was the last man to let his left hand know what his right was doing, there is every reason to believe he spent large sums in freeing the victims of misfortune and injustice among the debtors. And even when he was furthest from home, his letters were filled with the minutest directions to his steward for little kindnesses to his dependants, in which not even his horse was forgotten. Vast schemes of benevolence are well enough for staggering the imagination, but a faithfulness in these little kindnesses enriches

humanity at least as much. One likes the story of
the Dutch prisoner of war, whose unselfish labours
for the comfort of his fellow victims so impressed
Howard that he asked whether there was any way
in which he could serve him. The sailor at first
steadfastly affirmed his content with his lot, but
finally confessed that when at home his greatest
enjoyment was in a dish of tea. A week later a
small sugar loaf, a pound of tea and a tin kettle
arrived at the prison.

Howard must have had a particular fellow feeling
for this sailor, for his own solitary luxury was tea.
Otherwise his diet consisted solely of bread and
milk, fruit and vegetables. Thus he was a teeto-
taler and vegetarian, not on principle, for he was
no more bigoted in such matters than in others, but
because he believed that his own bodily needs were
best met by extremely simple fare.

Indeed, his tolerance and large-mindedness were
other characteristics which fitted him above other
men for his task. By education and choice he
belonged to the most unbending of the Puritan
sects, the Independents, yet he was not one of those
who thought he could best maintain his own beliefs
by decrying those of others. When at home he
frequently worshipped in his own parish church,
and was fast friends with his vicar. When abroad,
he was once asked if he was a Catholic, and replied,
" I love good people of all religions." He disliked
what he felt to be the superstition of the Roman
Church, and abhorred the Continental Sunday, yet
in Rome did not fear to speak with the man some
of his fellow sectarians knew as Anti-Christ. The

usual formalities were dispensed with at this visit,
and, after they had spent some time together, the
Pope, at parting, laid his hand on Howard's head,
saying, " I know you Englishmen set no value on
these things, but the blessing of an old man can do
you no harm."

It is hard to know upon which this brief meeting
reflected the greater credit, on the Pope who was
magnanimous enough to seek the interview, or the
Puritan who was magnanimous enough to welcome
it. The Spirit of Christ was in each of them, and
transcended the forms of man-made religion.

And indeed any consideration of Howard's character must end where it began, with the recognition
that it was above all his unceasing endeavour to live
in the knowledge and love of God that enabled him
to do and be what he was. Of this he was fully
conscious himself, as even a cursory survey of his
writings will show.

HOWARD AND THE PRISONS—EFFECT

The obvious way of estimating the effect of
Howard's work would be to put the problem in the
form of a sum and say that, the condition of the
prisons in 1774 having been subtracted from their
condition in 1790, the balance of improvement
should be credited to Howard, and labelled as his
contribution to prison reform.

Such improvements as had emerged were indeed
almost wholly due to Howard's efforts. He himself, in the last edition of his work, notes a progressive change for the better in many of the gaols

he visited. But there are also occasions where he
records a relapse, and sometimes positive retro-
gression, and it is well known that when the next
great reformer, Elizabeth Fry, came on the scenes,
conditions in the gaols were almost as bad as they
had been when Howard made his first journey.

As a result of such a reckoning, it has been
suggested that Howard is not really to be considered
as a reformer at all, but rather as a kind of self-
appointed committee of enquiry, which heard its
own evidence, and by reason of its constitution was
able for once to produce a really honest and uncompromising report. The value of this report is
fully recognised, both in regard to the matter it
contains, the manner of its presentment, and the
fact that it was the first of its kind, demonstrating
for all time the value of a searching and minute investigation as a preliminary to any kind of attempted
reform. But the preliminaries to reform and reform itself are different things, and as it is con-
tended that those alone who achieve the latter are
entitled to the name of reformers, that title has
been denied to Howard.

Such a contention (perhaps founded on Howard's
modest estimate of himself as " a plodder who went
about to collect material for men of genius to make
use of ") seems to involve a fundamental miscon-
ception of the part played by the reformer. It is
not his task to frame laws or get them passed. By
the time that part of the business is done, he
is usually dead, probably from overwork and dis-
disappointment, if not from martyrdom.

It is for the reformer to open men's eyes to

existing wrongs, inspire in them an active discontent and show them a vision of better things.

This Howard did in the matter of the prisons. He brought home to his law-abiding fellow-countrymen the neglected truth that his other law-breaking fellow-countrymen, though treated like beasts, were, in fact, human beings ; to use them otherwise was to degrade both them and their gaolers.

"Those gentlemen who, when they are told of the misery our prisoners suffer, content themselves with saying, let them keep out, prefaced perhaps with an angry prayer, seem not duly sensible of the favour of Providence which distinguishes them from the sufferers : they do not remember that we are required to imitate our gracious Heavenly Parent, who is *kind to the unthankful and to the evil* : they also forget the vicissitude of human affairs : the unexpected changes to which all men are liable ; and that those whose circumstances are affluent, may in time be reduced to indigence and become debtors and prisoners. And as to criminality, it is possible that a man who has often shuddered at hearing the account of a murder may, on sudden temptation, commit that very crime. *Let him that thinks he standeth take heed lest he fall* and commiserate those that are fallen."

"To reform prisoners . . . should always be the leading view in every house of correction . . . as *rational* and *immortal* beings we owe this to them ; nor can any criminality of things justify our neglect in this particular."

It was a new idea to consider criminals as rational and immortal beings. That its acceptance did not follow more rapidly was due to no fault of Howard. A glance at a history book will show the reason; no country which is fighting for its independence as a whole has time to consider the claims of a very small section. The war once over, Howard's disciples carried on his work and the Model Prison was evolved, bringing with it its own defects and inhumanities indeed, but sweeping away a vast majority of the grossest abuses of Howard's day.

Finally, Howard left behind the inspiration not merely of his ideas, but of his life. His single-minded, unswerving, unselfish devotion to his cause not only ennobles a rather sordid page in his country's social history, but enriches for all time the story of human achievement.

"I cannot name this gentleman without remarking that his labours and writings have done much to open the eyes and hearts of mankind. He has visited all Europe—not to survey the sumptuous-ness of palaces, or the stateliness of temples; not to make accurate measurements of the remains of ancient grandeur, nor to form a scale of the curiosity of modern art; not to collect medals or collate manuscripts—but to dive into the depths of dungeons and plunge into the infection of hospitals; to survey the mansions of sorrow and pain; to take the gauge and measure of misery, depression and contempt; to remember the forgotten, to attend to the neglected, to visit the forsaken, and compare and collate the miseries of all men in all countries. His plan is original; and it is full of genius as it is of humanity."

BURKE, *Speech at Bristol*, 1780.

WILLIAM WILBERFORCE (1759–1833)

By R. COUPLAND, M.A.

D

WILLIAM WILBERFORCE

I

In 1824 a little, frail old man passed for the last time through the doors of the House of Commons. Though his body, slender and stooping from youth up, was bent now (as his friends observed) into something like the letter S, he was not, in fact, so very old—not more than sixty-five—and any stranger who accosted him would have quickly forgotten the outward appearance of infirmity and noted only the almost youthful alertness and vivacity of the man, his simple courtesy and kindliness, and the singular sweetness of his expression. On the stage he was now quitting he had played a leading part for nearly forty years. In early days his beautiful voice had won him the title of " the nightingale of the House," and he had been one of its great orators in a great age of oratory. Nor was it merely in debate that he had ranked with his friends and contemporaries, Pitt and Fox and Burke. His political achievements had made him as famous in his way as they—and not in England only. With the possible exception of Wellington's, the name of William Wilberforce was now the best known and the most honoured British name throughout the world.

The cause of this fame was simple. While

Wellington had done as much as any other man to save the liberty of Europe from the despotism of Napoleon, Wilberforce had done more than any other man to save the liberty of the black races of mankind from the despotism of the white. The more the modern student ponders on what Wilberforce and his collaborators did, the more deeply impressed he must be by its magnitude. It transformed the relations between two, and in time between three, continents. It removed the most solid obstacle surviving from past ages to any general application of the Christian ideal to the relations between the diverse peoples of the world, to any practical hope of attaining unity and harmony on earth. It must be judged, therefore, to have been one of the greatest moral and social revolutions in history. In its full effects the abolition of the Slave Trade and Slavery was nothing less than that.

II

It is difficult nowadays to realise that less than a hundred years ago Slavery was a regular and respectable institution throughout the Western World. In most of the tropical dependencies of Great Britain, as in those of other European Powers, all the hard manual labour was done as a matter of course by negro slaves. In the eighteenth century slaves brought home for domestic service by colonial planters were a common sight in this country. There were over fourteen thousand of them here in 1772, when the judgment in the famous

Somerset case decided that the state of slavery could not exist in England. And for sixty years longer the state of slavery continued to exist—there was nothing in the law to prevent it—on English soil overseas. In 1830 there were at least 800,000 slaves in the ownership of British subjects.

Some of these slaves had been born in slavery; but, since the death-rate usually exceeded the birth-rate on the West Indian plantations, where most of them were domiciled, the great majority had been brought over the Atlantic from the western districts of Central Africa. It had been a terrible experience for them, this process of enslavement. Some of them had been kidnapped by the slave-traders. Some of them had been made prisoners by a neighbouring tribe whose chief had raided their village in order to make slaves and sell them for spirits or arms or gunpowder. Some of them had been condemned for offences which, with the same object in view, their chiefs had punished by enslavement. Then, men women and children herded in gangs, husbands torn from wives and wives from husbands and children from their parents, they had been marched to the coast, chained together, along rough tracks, their weaker comrades often dropping out to die by the way. And worse still had awaited them in the slave-ships. Packed flat between decks on shelves three feet apart, still in chains, and often so tight together that they could not turn round as they lay, terrified by their awful fate, by the unknown perils of the sea, and by fears of what new sufferings might yet await them, they had endured, almost like animals, the infernal " Middle Passage," a voyage of several weeks, in indescribable conditions of heat and filth and disease.   Many had died : some had seized a moment when they were allowed on deck for air and exercise, and when the often brutal seamen who looked after them were off their guard, to jump into the sea : it was frequently only three-quarters of the human cargo that had reached port.   Then, at last, came the slave-market and the appropriation of their persons—almost indeed of their lives—by individual masters.   Many of the masters, it is not always remembered, were humane. But many were not.   It was customary with some of them, for instance, to regard it as good business to work their slaves quickly to death and buy new ones.

It has been reckoned that from first to last the peoples of Europe carried twelve million Africans out of Africa into enslavement, and that about the same number of Africans perished in the process. Begun by the Portuguese in the fifteenth century, the Slave Trade had grown to vast proportions with the growth of European colonisation across the Atlantic.   The development of the English settlements on the southern coast of North America and in the West Indies in the seventeenth and eighteenth centuries had greatly increased the English share in it, till at last it became the lion's share.   In the years following the close of the American War in 1783, it was estimated that on an average about 74,000 slaves were exported every year from Africa, of which English ships carried 38,000, French 20,000, Portuguese 10,000, Dutch 4000, and Danish 2000.

To the modern mind these figures and all they stand for are astounding. We tend to forget the immense advance which civilised opinion has made in this humanitarian field. We cannot conceive how our ancestors, who were not so very different from ourselves, allowed the ghastly business to continue. But, of course, there were several solid reasons for it. To begin with, the realities of the exploitation of weak and coloured races by white and strong ones had not been forced on the attention of the English public; and it was difficult for the unimaginative Englishman to understand or trouble himself about the sufferings of strange and far-away folk. And most of those who did understand were, more or less uneasily, convinced by the strength of the case for the continuance of the evil. There were three main lines of argument. The colonial planters declared—and in those days it was generally accepted—that the plantation-colonies could not be maintained at all without slave-labour and therefore without the Slave Trade. "The impossibility of doing without slaves in the West Indies," wrote an English pamphleteer who was not without a conscience, "will always prevent this traffic being dropped. The necessity, the absolute necessity, then, of carrying it on must, since there is no other, be its excuse." The Englishmen engaged in the Trade, secondly, could point to the huge profits it brought into the country. Between 1783 and 1793 it paid on the average over thirty per cent. It has been described as "the most lucrative traffic the world has ever seen." The prosperity of the port of Liverpool, which took the largest part in the Trade, of Bristol too, and even of London, it was said, depended on it. And lastly came the politician's argument. Since England's naval power was so closely linked with her mercantile marine, it would be dangerous to leave so large a field of the carrying trade for less scrupulous rivals like France to occupy. Taken altogether it was a formidable case, and it was backed by the combined social and political influence of the planters and the merchants—the " West Indian " party—who wielded the same sort of power in Parliament and out of it as the " nabobs " of East Indian fame.

It is not, therefore, so surprising that, year after year, the evil thing went on. Protests, indeed, were made from time to time. Towards the end of the seventeenth century the Trade was denounced by Godwyn, an Anglican minister, and by Baxter, the great Nonconformist ; and in 1724 the Quakers began their long campaign against Slavery and the Trade together. Nor were these protests confined to the religious field. The negro began to figure in current literature. While the political writers of the eighteenth century were popularising the unhistorical idea of the virtuous state of nature and " the noble savage," Defoe was drawing his immortal picture of " Man Friday," and poets like Pope and Thomson were depicting the sacrifice of " poor Indians " and " Afric's sable children " to the " thirst for gold " and the " cruel trade." When, therefore, an appeal was made to the law, British opinion was in some degree prepared for it ; and the Somerset decision, obtained after more than one rebuff by the selfless exertions of the first " Abolitionist," Granville Sharp, and the similar Knight judgment in Scotland, were generally welcomed by public opinion. But Slavery still continued outside the British Isles, and the Slave Trade still fed it. The law as it stood permitted both ; the law could only be altered by Parliament, and nobody of influence in Parliament was yet prepared to combat that powerful case for accepting the inevitable. Outside its walls, in the period of the American War, the attack was carried on by such eminent men as Wesley, Adam Smith, Robertson, Paley, and Bishop Porteous ; but inside, Lord North commanded the general assent of the House of Commons when, in 1783, he politely rejected a petition from the Quakers against the Trade on the ground that it " had, in some measure, become necessary to almost every nation in Europe."

But the cause of the backward peoples, whether in Africa or in India, was no longer a field for the intermittent activities of occasional idealists. The new humanitarianism was a definite, persistent " movement," not easily to be discouraged. In the course of the next few years a Committee for the Abolition of the Slave Trade was formed, with a group of Quakers for its kernel, with Granville Sharp as its chairman, and with Clarkson, a young Cambridge man who had determined to devote his life to the cause, and Ramsay, who had seen Slavery at close quarters in the West Indies, as its most vigorous members. By themselves, however, this little band could scarcely hope to achieve their end. How could men relatively so little known appeal effectively to the conscience of the nation ? How

could they educate and excite the British public
to the overthrow of so great and old a " vested
interest " ?   How could they win over a majority
in either House of Parliament—that necessary
majority if anything practical was really to be done
—or how enlist the ministerial support without
which that majority was obviously unattainable ?
What they needed was a politician for their leader,
a politician of great gifts and high standing, one
who could catch the ear of Parliament, however
unpopular his theme ; who could safely and effectively appeal to the country at large, even on a
purely moral issue, and, last but not least, whose
opinion would have weight in Government circles.
In 1787 they found him.

One day in that year, three friends sat talking
under an old oak which still stands on the ridge
above the vale of Keston, near the village of Hol-
wood in Kent.   Their names were Pitt, Grenville,
and Wilberforce.   The subject of their talk was a
suggestion made by Pitt and backed by Grenville
that Wilberforce should take up the question of the
Slave Trade in Parliament ; and its upshot was a
decision on Wilberforce's part which in the end
did more than anything else to bring about the
abolition not only of the Slave Trade, but of
Slavery itself.

III

If the suggestion had been made to Wilberforce
a few years earlier, it is more than probable that
nothing would have come of it.   To lead a cam-

paign against the Slave Trade might well seem a desperate course for any politician. He would have to work very hard to master the details of the subject. He would incur the bitter enmity of the West Indians and all their "hangers-on." He would be derided as a fanatic and slandered as something worse. He would get no help from either political party : indeed, the adoption of such an idealistic cause might well wreck his parliamentary career. And the prospects of his succeeding in the end would be very meagre. It might seem, in fact, to be almost a forlorn hope. Despite his hatred of cruelty and oppression, Burke had shied away from it, and Fox, too, despite his love of freedom and humanity. Almost certainly Wilberforce —a few years earlier—would have reckoned up the difficulties like those other and older men, and, like them, passed by on the other side.

For Wilberforce, at the end of 1784, was not distinguished from his friends by any particular moral earnestness or fortitude. Born of a wealthy commercial family in Hull, he had quickly gained a footing in the brilliant little world of London Society. His social graces—his winning manners, his unfailing amiability, his love of fun, his gifts of song and mimicry—had made him a favourite with everybody. And his diary bears witness to the whirl of fashionable gaiety in which he moved throughout the London season — dances and "routs" till the small hours, evenings at the opera or the play, suppers with Mrs Siddons or Mrs Crewe, dinner-parties with duchesses, card-parties at one or other of his five clubs. This life of pleasure taxed his delicate health, but it never soiled him. He had no taste, indeed, for the uglier vices of the day ; and there is a touch of the older Wilberforce in his sudden decision to give up gambling because of its danger to poorer men than himself. Meanwhile, he had become as notable and popular a figure in politics as in Society. In his early days in London he had formed an intimate and lasting friendship with the younger Pitt, his exact contemporary ; he had obtained a seat in the House of Commons in the same year, 1780 ; and thenceforward, through the exciting days of the American War, the opposition to the North-Fox coalition, and the beginning of the youthful Pitt's long premiership, he had enthusiastically backed his friend with voice and vote. If his gifts were not yet mature enough to win him a place in the Cabinet, he could render no small service to the Government by his eloquence in debate ; and, on his election for Yorkshire in 1784, he became one of the most important persons in the House. Yet, however successful, however important, he felt no serious call in politics. It was something like a game, a very enjoyable intellectual game, one of the most pleasant of the many pleasant occupations which were open to a well-to-do English gentleman of the eighteenth century.

And then, in 1785, the whole of Wilberforce's life was changed. In the previous autumn—he was then twenty-five—he had travelled to the French Riviera with Isaac Milner, with whom he had become closely acquainted when the latter was a schoolmaster at Hull at the beginning of his distinguished career as mathematician and divine. Milner had been deeply affected by that tremendous religious upheaval of the later eighteenth century, the Evangelical movement ; and in the course of their journey he persuaded Wilberforce to read Doddridge's *Rise and Progress of Religion.* It made a profound impression on the gay young man's receptive mind. The next summer he travelled again with Milner, and now they read the New Testament in Greek together. " By degrees," wrote Wilberforce long afterwards, " I imbibed his sentiments, though I must confess with shame that they long remained merely as opinions assented to by my understanding but not influencing my heart." Already, however, the change was detected by some of his fashionable friends whom he met at Spa. " Mrs Crewe," he notes in his diary, " cannot believe that I can think it wrong to go to the play." And during the autumn the process of " conversion " moved fast to its climax. The private journal of his inner life, which Wilberforce began to keep at this time besides his diary, bears witness that he suffered to the full the bitter pains of the Evangelical penitent. " I must awake to my dangerous state, and never be at rest till I have made my peace with God." " My heart is so hard, my blindness so great, that I cannot get a due hatred of sin." For months he was sunk " in the deepest depression from strong conviction of my guilt." He shunned society. He took his name off all his clubs. He saw little or nothing of his old friends, even of intimates like Pitt. But, at last, having sought the spiritual advice of the Rev. John Newton

—once an outcast on the African coast, later the captain of a slave-ship, and now a fiery prophet of the flames of Hell in the pulpit of St Mary Woolnoth—Wilberforce emerged from his misery ; and, though for the rest of his life he continued to scan his every thought and deed and to lament his negligences and backslidings, he recovered something like his old happy spirit, or, rather, as he put it, a " serenity, tranquillity, composure which is not to be destroyed."

For politics, however, or at least for party-politics, he seemed to have lost all taste ; and at the end of the year he wrote to his old political comrade and chief to tell him so. Pitt was dismayed—not merely, be it said, because of the loss to his party, but mainly lest it should mean that Wilberforce, for whom he had a warm affection, was going to turn his back on the world and become a religious recluse. He insisted on a candid talk. Wilberforce reluctantly consented. And though they failed to agree on the deeper principles at issue, Pitt's earnest plea that an active interest in public affairs was part of a Christian's duty had probably some effect. At any rate Wilberforce soon returned to the House of Commons ; and there he found himself able, without offending his new conscience, to support the mild measures of retrenchment and reform with which Pitt was nursing his country back to health after the disaster of the American War. But the life had gone out of it. He could not fight for the Government with any of his old enthusiasm. He could no longer breathe the tainted atmosphere of personal ambition, of "influence" and corruption, which still hung so thick round party-politics. If only some great issue should arise, transcending party-strife—an unmistakable challenge to the right against the wrong, a clear call to a Christian warrior, a crusade! But was there such an issue? For a time Wilberforce felt drawn to a campaign against vice, and he took a leading part in forming a Society which busied itself with the suppression of indecent and blasphemous publications and similar activities. But this was not enough to fill Wilberforce's life; and he was, so to speak, prepared and waiting when presently the clear call came. No particular person seems to have been responsible for turning his mind towards the Slave Trade. Wilberforce himself spoke afterwards of "many impulses which were all giving to my mind the same direction." But when, before long, he realised that the cause of the negroes was indeed the cause he sought, he had no doubt whence the determining "impulse" came. The suppression of the Slave Trade was an object—so he wrote in his journal—which "God Almighty has set before me."

IV

Wilberforce was soon to discover the need for this unfailing spiritual "impulse." At first, it is true, the task he had set himself seemed not so supremely difficult after all. The period between 1787 and 1793 was in some respects just the right period for just such a crusade. In the first place, the ground had been prepared, as has already been noticed, by the first humanitarian attacks on Slavery and the Trade and by the spread of new ideas in England and in France—new ideas not only about the virtues of " savage " peoples, but also about the value of human individuality and the natural equality of man and man.   And, secondly, the reaction from the spiritual passivity of the earlier eighteenth century was now in full swing among a large section of the English people. Many Englishmen were passionately preoccupied, almost obsessed, with the thought of sin.   And the conception of the Slave Trade as a great national sin—so Wilberforce always described it and so indeed it was—appealed at once to the popular imagination, and produced in the public mind something akin to the individual penitent's remorse.   It was a period, moreover, when English politics were once more moving along liberal lines.   Peace was expected to last for many years.   Prosperity, already wonderfully restored, promised to endure and to increase.   It was a good time for overhauling the body politic and redressing any ills that might be detected therein.   Reform, in fact, was in the air. And so those Englishmen who were not easily susceptible to the new religious " enthusiasm "— the dominant aristocracy, the world of culture and learning, the country gentlemen who filled the benches of the House of Commons—were ready to listen to Wilberforce's grim recital of the horrors of the Trade and to allow their natural human sympathies for once to impinge on the field of practical politics and commerce.

Despite, therefore, the weight and variety of argument brought forward by the champions of the Trade, when, after careful preparation, Wilberforce opened his campaign in 1789, it was evident at once that the cause of Abolition had strong support in Parliament and in the country. Pitt could not make it a Government measure, because his Cabinet and his party were not agreed on it ; but he warmly supported Wilberforce. So did Fox and Burke and a substantial minority in the House of Commons. In 1790 the terrible facts were displayed in formal evidence at the bar. In 1791 a second great debate raised the Abolitionist vote to half of that of the majority. In 1792, through the zealous efforts of Clarkson and others, an organised movement—the first of its kind in politics—was set on foot throughout the country and petitions against the Trade poured in at Westminster. The subsequent debate was at least half successful. Pitt made one of the finest speeches of his career ; and the House voted by 238 to 85, not indeed for instant Abolition, but for gradual Abolition, which was interpreted to mean the cessation of the Trade in 1796. If nothing had occurred to interrupt the normal course of politics, there can be little doubt that this resolution would have been confirmed by statute in the course of the next few years : and if a reform so great in its effects and opposed by such powerful interests had actually been carried within ten years, it would have been a wonderful achievement. But in fact it took twice as long.

Every one knows how the outbreak in 1793 of the long war with the French Revolution and Napoleon

E

checked the tide of liberalism in England, and imposed on every field of English politics a period of reaction and negation which lasted till the late 'twenties of the next century. And of all liberal causes none suffered more severely than the cause of Abolition. Like the others, it suffered from anti-Jacobinism, from the fear of liberty in England inspired by licence in France, from the obsession of the public mind with the bogey of internal unrest and later with the more solid danger of Napoleon. But it also suffered in four special ways. First, the application of the new French theories led to a ghastly struggle between blacks and whites in St Domingo, and, the infection spreading, there was some unrest and one or two small and ineffective risings among the slaves in the neighbouring British West Indies. Secondly, the argument against doing anything to weaken British shipping and sea power was greatly strengthened by the war. Thirdly, the British command of the sea meant that the British share in the Trade and in the profits thereof was greatly increased. And lastly—and perhaps more fatally—Pitt's support of Abolition, so essential to its success, and at first so sincere and energetic, began to weaken, as the burden of the struggle with Napoleon, which lay so heavily on him that in the end it killed him, filled his thoughts and impaired his strength. Under all these circumstances it is not in the least surprising that the resolution of 1792 was not implemented and that the cause of Abolition seemed at least as hopeless as the cause of Parliamentary Reform. What is surprising is that Wilberforce, unlike most of his friends and even of his collaborators, never ceased to hope and, more, to fight. Session after session, he continued his appeal to the conscience of the Commons by proposing Abolitionist motions : the war itself, he pleaded, was an urgent reason for the nation to free itself of guilt in the eyes of God. Year after year, he went on studying the subject, reviewing old evidence, obtaining new, talking always and everywhere about it, importuning the weary Pitt, winning fresh converts in society, and all at the cost of his comfort, his health, and even, at times, his safety. His concentration on one subject not directly concerned with the war was regarded by many as unpatriotic, by some as almost Jacobin. Old friends grew cold. At Court, in Society, in Parliament, he was slighted, reprobated, ridiculed. He was pursued by the enmity of the less respectable " West Indians." Calumnies were spread abroad about his private morals. His life was threatened by more than one truculent " slaver." But neither unpopularity nor abuse nor threats deterred him for a moment from his patient unresting labour. It may well be questioned if any social or political crusader has ever shown a more selfless devotion, a more stubborn perseverance than Wilberforce throughout those years of war. But to Wilberforce himself there was nothing at all remarkable in it. When doubting friends suggested that the cause might be shelved till the war was over, he had a simple answer—" When the actual commission of guilt is in question, a man who fears God is not at liberty."

And at last he had his reward. The death of

Pitt in 1806 and the accession to office of a Coalition Government, including Fox, transformed the polical situation as to the Abolition issue.   Fox, unlike Pitt, hated the Trade at least as much as he feared Napoleon ; and the Cabinet in which he served was the first Cabinet which contained no whole-hearted opponent of Abolition.   In the summer of 1806 Fox himself moved a resolution, purposely framed in similar terms to those of Wilberforce's resolutions in past years, and carried it by a great majority. He died a few months later, but the cause was already won.   In 1807 a Bill was enacted by which the Slave Trade was " utterly abolished, prohibited, and declared to be unlawful."

In the debates in both Houses the leading speakers vied with each other in ascribing the main credit for this final triumph of the cause to Wilberforce, and in the Commons he received a tumultuous ovation.   Nor was it in Parliament only that men recognised and applauded the greatness of his achievement.   Throughout England, and not least in his native Yorkshire, he was enrolled in the immortal company of famous men.   But the triumph and the fame made no change at all in Wilberforce.   He was still the modest, unassuming, gentle-mannered, attractive little man that he had always been.   He seems, indeed, to have thought little of himself save as an instrument in the hands of " the Giver of all good."

V

The destruction of the British Slave Trade, if the greatest, was not by any means the last of Wilberforce's achievements. In 1807 he was only forty-eight; he lived to be seventy-three; and the second period of his life was filled by an increasing stream of work and of influence in British and indeed in world affairs. To begin with, the Slave Trade did not end when Britain withdrew from it; and it was largely due to Wilberforce's insistent agitation that British public opinion was brought to bear on international diplomacy in favour of universal abolition. As a result, when, at the close of the war, the statesmen of Europe gathered to construct the basis of a new age of peace, the one supreme object which an ardent and unanimous electorate charged the British representatives to pursue was Abolition. Such pressure from the powerful nation which had played the chief part in freeing Europe from Napoleon could not long be resisted. By 1818 all the maritime Powers had followed the British lead or promised to do so in a few years' time; and, though it was still many years before it was finally and completely enforced by joint naval action against smugglers, the law of every civilised state forbade the bestial traffic before the nineteenth century was half-way through. And in the course of those international negotiations Wilberforce became an international figure. All the world regarded this gentle, pious, but pertinacious Englishman as the champion-in-chief of the negro peoples.

An eminent Italian called him " the Washington of humanity."

Meantime he had acquired an immense prestige in his own country. Public opinion is quick to detect and to honour unselfish public service ; and, if Wilberforce had his critics, if some thought him too much of a fanatic and others too much of a Tory, no one ever suggested that he sought his own profit or power, just as no one ever suggested that his piety was hypocritical. There can be no doubt in fact that his selflessness and his piety had a very wide influence on contemporary English life. His house was beset by visitors—many of them strangers seeking advice and help that were never refused—and everybody who came into personal contact with him was impressed by the earnestness and sincerity of his spiritual life. Cynics may have smiled at some of his ways—his constant references to the divine ordering of the world, his deliberate attempts to lead the conversation at social gatherings to the discussion of higher things, his strict observance of the Sabbath—but none of them seems to have derided or disliked him. It is remarkable that his fashionable friends, including the notorious Prince Regent, made a point of modifying the customary grossness of their talk when Wilberforce was present. Such tributes would never have been paid him if he had been a hypocrite or a prig. And in truth he was nothing like either. He was too human and too sincere—human enough to avoid the besetting sins of the conventional Puritan, to be good without being dull, to abstain from amusements he disliked without seeming to censure others for partaking in them, to retain till the end his unconquerably youthful spirit and his inexhaustible kindliness of heart; and sincere enough to spend hours of his busy time in secret, earnest, and often remorseful meditation, to deny himself all a rich man's luxuries, to spend a quarter of his income and sometimes to cut into his capital for charity, and, when faced with the prospect of death, as he was more than once, to blame himself for feeling " no ardour or warmth." He was not a hypocrite, nor a prig, nor a crank, nor a pietist. He was, surely, a saint.

And indeed, when he and his little group of friends in Parliament were given the nickname of " The Saints," there was no sarcasm or derision in it. They were too well-known and too much respected for the pettier barbs of politics to be worth using against them. Granville Sharp (till his death in 1818), Charles Grant and his son (Lord Glenelg), John Shore (Lord Teignmouth), Henry Thornton, James Stephen, John Venn, Zachary Macaulay—to name only the most eminent—these were a notable body of men, most of them wealthy but giving generously away, all of them busy in their various fields of work but spending all their leisure in some form of public service, linked together by intermarriage and by living for the most part in the same suburban village—whence their second nickname, " The Clapham Sect "—and wielding by their community of aim and by the combined effect of their reputations a great influence on politics and public opinion. The voice of " The Saints " in Parliament was anxiously awaited and seriously weighed : no Government could afford to disregard it. In fact, this little body of religious politicians, led by Wilberforce, speaking and voting only as conscience bade them, was as important and useful an element in British public life as it was unique. There has been nothing like it since.

VI

Few men have ever carried so heavy a responsibility as the leader of the " Clapham Sect." Except, as will be seen, in certain Radical circles, Wilberforce's moral authority was almost unquestioned. He was regarded as the keeper of the nation's conscience. And since his power was therefore so great, it is not unnatural to examine closely the use he made of it and to wonder, perhaps, if he did all the good he might have done. Apart from the negro question his main interests and activities were devoted to the religious field and especially to mission-work. No one took a more ardent or more effective share than he in the great expansion of overseas missionary enterprise in this period. He was one of the founders of the Church Missionary Society and of the British and Foreign Bible Society. No organisation of " good works " was complete without his patronage ; at any philanthropic meeting his presence on the platform was almost a matter of course. And all this side of his life took a great deal of time : it meant a huge correspondence and innumerable personal interviews. None the less, Wilberforce never neglected his Parliamentary duties. Quite apart from his prestige and from the particular respect that was paid to his opinion, he was, as representing Yorkshire, one of the most important members of the House of Commons ; and, despite its ill effects on his health, he made a point of regular attendance. Nor was he unaware of his peculiar responsibility. He laboured anxiously, and never without prayer, to judge truly the many controversial issues which distracted and embittered public life from 1807 till his retirement in 1824.

To one political party the results of these conscientious efforts gave little satisfaction. The Radicals declared that Wilberforce always pretended to have an open mind, to be a " crossbencher " without any party allegiance, and then always spoke and voted for the Tories. And there was some truth in the charge. Wilberforce's politics had been set into a permanent mould by his early devotion to Pitt. After his " conversion," it is true, he was never again a consistent, still less a militant, party man. But he had been the first of the " Pittites," and, despite occasional differences even on the supreme issue of war and peace, he remained a Pittite till his hero's death, and afterwards till his own. That meant that he was a Tory, not indeed of the Eldon brand, but like the pre-war Pitt or Canning or Huskisson. And this Toryism, moderate though it was and not so very different from contemporary Whiggism, implied at the best a negative attitude on the most vital domestic question of the time—the condition of the innocent and inevitable victims of the economic results of the war and the industrial revolution. On the political aspect of the problem of poverty the impartial student cannot but regret that Wilberforce was one of the great majority of his class who failed to recognise that the agitation inspired by destitution and discontent aimed only at Reform and not at Revolution; that, like most of his friends, he was afraid of Jacobinism in England; that, as he accepted Pitt's *régime* of repression, so he accepted Sidmouth's. And there were other reasons for this passive acquiescence. He was influenced by the dominant economic doctrine of *laissez-faire* and, still more deeply, by a doctrine of " other-worldliness," common enough at that time in his Evangelical school, which accepted poverty as part of God's dispensation, and minimised the ills as well as the goods of this transitory life on earth as compared with the eternal felicity of grace and salvation. But such motives could be no excuse to the Radicals. The greater Wilberforce's moral authority, the more odious seemed to them his Toryism. Must a sufferer have a black skin, they asked, to enlist the sympathy of the world-famed champion of humanity ? Quick haters like Cobbett hated Wilberforce; Hazlitt drew a rancorous portrait of him in the *Spirit of the Age*; and, not unnaturally perhaps, but rather unfairly, historians of English social life, necessarily concentrating on the economic question, have sometimes tended to over-emphasise—not always without a sneer—this failure of Wilberforce to help the English poor.

To allow that issue to colour one's whole picture

of Wilberforce would involve, of course, an almost grotesque loss of balance and proportion. In the first place it would wholly ignore the liberal side of Wilberforce's politics—his appeals for the public relief of poverty and for state-employment, his demands for popular education, his persistent attacks on the old-time severities of the Penal Code and especially the Game Laws, his denunciations of the Transportation system and the condition of English prisons, his support of factory legislation on behalf of the children, his plea for the wretched little chimney-sweeps. Moreover, on the two major issues outside economics, Wilberforce was more of a Whig than a Tory : he was in favour of Roman Catholic emancipation in Ireland and for at any rate a moderate measure of Parliamentary Reform. But the second line of defence—if defence is needed—is the more obvious and conclusive. Wilberforce was not, he never pretended to be, an all-round statesman. He was a crusader in a single cause—the cause of the millions of African peoples ; and, since his intellectual and constructive ability was by no means extraordinary and since his physical strength was by no means unlimited, it was only by giving far the greater part of his time and thought and energy to this particular crusade that he was able to carry it to victory. Could more be expected of any one man ? Is it not, indeed, a kind of tribute to the magnitude of what Wilberforce did when his critics complain of what he did not do ?

VII

The abolition of the Slave Trade was only the first part of Wilberforce's work; the second part was the abolition of Slavery itself.

Wilberforce never forgot what his cause owed to his collaborators. He was well aware that the work of Granville Sharp, Clarkson, Ramsay, Macaulay, Babington, and others had been as essential for success as his own. And with regard to the abolition of Slavery this was even more obvious than with regard to the abolition of the Trade, for the simple reason that, long before the end was attained, Wilberforce had been compelled by age and infirmity to retire from active life, and Buxton had assumed the leadership in his place. But the victory over Slavery was more than half won by the victory over the Trade. From the outset, indeed, the Abolitionists realised that the two evils were closely interlinked; and it was only as a matter of strategy and not of principle that they made their first assault on the Trade alone. The campaign, however, inevitably told almost as heavily against Slavery itself. It opened Englishmen's eyes to the sufferings of the negroes: it roused their conscience and awakened their sympathy: and, as the story of cruelty and oppression was unfolded, it became clear that those evils were not confined only to the period of the slave's life in which he figured as an article of trade. Slavery, on the other hand, as the emancipators had always foreseen, was a more formidable object of attack than the Trade. The question of its abolition instantly raised the principle, so dear to the English and especially to the legal mind, of the rights of property. Abolition meant nothing short of confiscation. It also raised the principle of self-government. Whereas an ocean trade might well be regarded as a matter for the Imperial Government's control, slavery on the plantations was surely a matter for the planters to deal with in their own little island parliaments. Material interests, furthermore, seemed more widely involved. If Slavery itself, and not the Trade only, were to be abolished, the prophecies of economic disaster for the West Indies could be uttered with more conviction and more truth. And, lastly, a much better case could be made even on the negro's behalf for Slavery than for the Trade. There was no escaping the horrors of the latter : efforts to improve its conditions had been tried and had failed. But the sufferings of many of the slaves were over, once the hideous voyage was done. Many of the planters—as Wilberforce repeatedly confessed —were humane, considerate men ; and on many of the plantations the slaves were certainly better cared for and may perhaps have been happier than in the barbarous freedom of their old homes in Africa.

It is remarkable, then, that the second campaign, which formally opened in 1823 and ended in victory ten years later, should have been relatively so short. Or rather it would be remarkable if so much of the work had not been done before, if the great tide of public feeling, raised so high by the first campaign, had not been ready to sweep on and overwhelm the objective of the second.   The story cannot be told within the limits of this essay.[1] Suffice it to say here that the main obstacle lay not in Parliament nor in England but in the West Indies ; that the end would have come in far less than a decade if successive British Governments had not tried again and again, and always vainly, to persuade the colonial legislatures to do their unpleasant duty themselves ; and that only after years of wasted patience, and even then only under vigorous pressure from Buxton and his colleagues, the Whig Ministry of Lord Grey and the Reform Act braced their shoulders and did the deed.

During the closing years of the campaign, the old crusader who had led it at the outset was living in retirement, enjoying the peace and rest of his evening, as serene and young-hearted and affectionate as he had always been, constantly casting his mind gratefully back to the providential turning-point of his life in 1785, complaining only that he had been " an unprofitable servant."   But, outside the battle though he was, Wilberforce still played a part in winning it.   To Buxton, whom he chose as his successor, and to all Buxton's allies, the thought of Wilberforce's example, the intense personal devotion they felt towards him, his unflagging interest in the progress of the struggle, his encouragement, and, at need, his advice—all this was an unfailing inspiration.   And on the battlefield itself—in Parliament—the memory of Wilberforce was in all men's minds.

[1] It has been admirably told by Mr W. L. Mathieson in *British Slavery and its Abolition* (Longmans, 1926).

It so happened that the veteran's last illness in 1833 coincided with the passage of the Abolition Bill through the House of Commons. " When Mr Wilberforce hears of it," said Lord Stanley, the Bill's official author, in the course of the debate, "he may well exclaim, ' Lord, now lettest Thou Thy servant depart in peace.' " And when indeed Wilberforce was informed that the Bill was safe and that its passage had been eased by a generous grant to compensate the planters, " Thank God," he said, " that I should have lived to witness a day in which England is willing to give twenty millions sterling for the abolition of Slavery." Four days later he died. A year later eight hundred thousand slaves were freed.

" The unweary, unostentatious, and inglorious crusade of England against Slavery," wrote Lecky, a cool, reflective historian, " may probably be regarded as among the three or four perfectly virtuous pages comprised in the history of nations." If so great a tribute can be fairly paid to the England of a century ago, and if the England of to-day can still be inspired by the ideals then implanted in her national tradition, it is Wilberforce's doing more than that of any other man. And that Wilberforce did it was mainly due to the substance and the strength of his Christian faith.

Note.—The historical materials on which this essay has been based may be found in *Wilberforce, a Narrative,* by R. Coupland (Oxford, 1923).

LORD SHAFTESBURY

ANTHONY ASHLEY COOPER
SEVENTH EARL OF SHAFTESBURY
(1801-85)

By CONSTANCE SMITH, O.B.E.

F

SHAFTESBURY

A RUNNING leap backward through half a dozen centuries often needs less effort of the imagination than the standing jump over a hundred years. When the whole scene—political, economic, religious—shifts at once, the change is too violent to fail of its effect on the human mind ; the newness and strangeness of the general view helps to compel attention to unfamiliar detail. In a survey of social conditions under, say, Richard II. we expect to be surprised, startled, shocked, and are on the watch for facts which will provide the anticipated sensations. It is otherwise when the approach is to a period only just out of reach in time, which shows superficially the marks of our own age and is yet utterly remote from it in every habit of thought bearing upon corporate life and national responsibility. To bridge the gulf between our present-day tasks and those of the social reformer of the early nineteenth century we have to reconstruct mentally a vanished world : the world of individualism unashamed and highly exalted, watching with intoxicated delight the forward march of the New Industry, terrified—in Parliament and outside it—of any suggestion of interference with the mechanism of an economic scheme of things which could only, according to general belief, maintain its equipoise in an atmosphere of un-

checked *laissez-faire* ; philosophically satisfied that
grinding poverty, degrading conditions of life,
unhealthy and brutalising conditions of labour, high
death-rates and epidemic disease and deformity
were the necessary portion of a large part of the
community, to be accepted like the law of gravitation.   In such a world, in the year after the passing
of the Reform Bill and the General Election of
1832, Ashley, taking charge of the Ten Hours Bill
left fatherless by Sadler's recent loss of his seat at
Leeds, began his labours on behalf of the factory
worker.

He was then in his thirty-second year, and had
already sat for six years in the House of Commons.
His seat in Parliament and his office under Government (he had been a Commissioner of the Board
of India Control from 1828 until the Tory Government was defeated at the Reform Bill election of
1831) had come to him as a matter of course in
the political circumstances of the time.   But the
capacity and industry he showed as a member of
the India Board, like his first class at Oxford, had
given some indication of powers not necessarily
present in the representative of a ducal pocket
borough ; moreover, he had already shown that he
had a mind open to receive evidence of the existence of abuses and eager to remedy them where
they were proved real.

His first important speech was delivered as
seconder of Robert Gordon's motion to bring in
a Bill for the amendment of Lunacy Law, and
when the delegates of the Short Time Committees
approached him he had been four years an unpaid

Commissioner in Lunacy. A young man who in 1828 was ready to espouse the cause of the most helpless and neglected members of the community —creatures regarded, according to the temperament of the observer, with amusement as grotesque " shows " or with repulsion as uncanny horrors to be thrust out of sight and forgotten—might fitly have suggested himself to Bull and his colleagues as first choice for the succession to Sadler. Actually, it was only after repeated failure to obtain the help they needed in other quarters that the delegates accepted Sir Andrew Agnew's advice that they should apply to Ashley. Ashley himself has recorded in his diary the " astonishment and doubt and terror " with which he received their unexpected request. His knowledge of the factory question was confined to certain extracts from the evidence given before Sadler's Committee and published in *The Times*—he had heard neither Sadler's great speech on the Ten Hours Bill nor the earlier debates on the subject—but these statements had so " astonished and disgusted " him that he was moved, after the champion's defeat, to write and offer his services " for any small work the cause might require." Now he found himself suddenly confronted with a call to fill the leader's place. He begged for time to reflect, but any delay would have left the door open for the introduction of the blocking Bill Morpeth was known to have in readiness, and decision by the following morning was required of him. He consulted two friends, who both counselled a favourable answer, went home, meditated and prayed, and decided on acceptance of the task which was to occupy the best years of his life.

His fitness for that task was both individual and relative. Hatred of wickedness, cruelty, and oppression of the weak was a part of his nature : he kindled to indignation at the bare report of such things. But his indignation was not the fierce flame that dies down when the hot word has been spoken or the rush of impulsive action is over ; it was a steady-burning fire that, even when circumstances had damped it down for years, kept its central heat and sprang to life again at the first breath of the outer air. His courage was unflinching, but even more remarkable was his power of perseverance. Almost every reform he undertook required nearly a generation of labour before the goal was reached. His few sympathisers and helpers in Parliament were, like himself, lone figures confronting a coalition army in which such high-minded statesmen as Graham and Peel, and reformers in other spheres like Bright and Cobden, opposed them with as much determination as the outraged representatives of the " manufacturing interest " and the mass of back-benchers to whom State interference was anathema. Outside the House of Commons there were not many with whom he could work closely and continuously : Chartism confused the issue in one direction, trade unionism—from which he held aloof as a dangerous force—in another. Conservative in principle and outlook, he sought to set bounds to factory reform which we can see to have been plainly impossible— bounds already overleaped by Fielden as a reforming employer. But then Fielden was in touch with factory problems and factory workers within the walls of his own mill ; Ashley, at the outset, viewed them from a distance.

He did his best to overcome that drawback by frequent visits to factory districts, by first-hand observation of the abuses he sought to remedy and personal contact with the operatives. In this way he gained much knowledge. But by temperament, tradition and education he remained an aristocrat ; to the end he worked *for* rather than *with* the people whose cause he championed. It was not a simple matter for this proud, reserved and sensitive man to work on equal terms with anybody. That lonely and unhappy childhood, of which the outcome was an unquenchable passion of pity for all suffering children, had sealed in him the springs of geniality and easy intercourse with his fellows. In fairness it should also be remembered that the operative of the first half of the nineteenth century, without political power, frequently without education, without knowledge (save in a few exceptional cases) of how reform could be brought about, was not the kind of person whom he would naturally draw into consultation at every step of the difficult road. A born leader of men, with a leader's gift of tact and insight, would have known how to get at the mind of the inarticulate worker and translate it for him into terms which made practical comradeship possible. Ashley had very little insight and no tact ; and he was not a leader, except of forlorn hopes which had a curious way of being successful at long last.

Yet, despite his limitations—in a sense because of them—the Short Time Committees chose their man well. A hostile Parliament, a contemptuous or indifferent public was more likely to respond to the arguments of a man of rank and position than to those of any member of the newly-enfranchised middle class. The workman, still regarded by politicians as an indistinguishable unit of the voteless but dangerous masses, would in 1833 have got no hearing at all. Moreover, it counted on the whole in Ashley's favour that he was, as the late Lord Salisbury said of Mr Gladstone, " a great Christian." In spite of taunts of " cant " flung across the floor of the House of Lords, no one ever really doubted the strength and sincerity of his religion ; and in the England of 1833 the force of the Evangelical revival was still at flood-tide and the preaching of John Wesley a deeply-cherished memory.

When Ashley opened the first of his campaigns on behalf of Ten Hours in 1833 the omens seemed favourable. He introduced Sadler's Bill into a House of Commons which, for all the great change that had passed over it, kept some memory of the terrible evidence given before Sadler's Committee, and was inclined to agree that the fixing of nine years as the minimum age of employment and ten hours' work a day for everyone under eighteen constituted reasonable reforms. But the men of the new Whig Government, of whom Althorp, Leader of the House, was the type and exponent, were saturated with the prevailing economic doctrine, and the representatives of employers were spoiling

for a fight. At first, when the latter clamoured for
a Commission, alleging that Sadler's Committee
had reported unfairly, the Ministerial spokesmen
temporised and hesitated, but they ended by
giving way. By a majority of one the Commission
was appointed.

Its appointment was extraordinarily unpopular
in the country. The Commissioners themselves,
sitting in London, suffered many attacks in speech
and writing; their investigators in the industrial
areas encountered the full fury of the storm. It
was taken for granted that the object of their visits
was to build up a case against the Bill, and they were
received in towns like Huddersfield, Leeds and
Bradford with outbursts of public feeling expressing
itself in crowded indignation meetings, the adoption
of resolutions bitterly hostile to their enquiry, and
processions of children chanting insistent demands
for the Ten Hours Bill. No doubt these demon-
strations were carefully organised. They had the
worst effect on the minds of the Commissioners,
who put it on record in their Report that the
working men of the North were the victims and
dupes of hired agitators, who had already induced
them to call for a Ten Hours Bill which must have
the disastrous effect of limiting the labour of adult
persons, and were now inducing them to believe that
their position could be improved by combination
in trade unions. The pretended pity of these
agitators for the children was pure propaganda.

While the Commissioners had been enquiring
and reporting, Ashley had carried the second
reading of his Bill and successfully defeated a

proposal that it should be referred to a Select Committee. But there was no future for it. The Commissioners had effectually killed all inclination for so drastic a reform as a Ten Hours day promoted by "hired agitators." The House accepted an amendment, based on the Commissioners' recommendation, to reduce the age of protection from eighteen to thirteen, and Ashley handed over his maimed Bill to the Government.

Then a curious thing happened. Ministers were anxious to do as little as possible. Ordinary members of Parliament, assured on high medical authority that the procession of diseased, deformed and stunted creatures, exhausted at seventeen, old at twenty, which had passed before Sadler's Committee, owed their miseries to over-employment in early childhood, and that fourteen hours' daily labour in the factory was "comparatively easy" to boys and girls of thirteen, acquiesced in the official view. Neither seem to have understood that the proposals of the Commissioners themselves constituted a large advance on previous factory legislation. The Act of 1833, in which they were embodied, brought under regulation for the first time woollen, worsted, hemp, flax, tow, linen and silk mills, and forbade the employment in all of them—silk only excepted—of any child under nine, and set up a forty-eight hour week for children under thirteen. It limited the labour of young persons under eighteen to twelve in the day and sixty-nine in the week, and prescribed a daily allowance of one and a half hours for meals, making a period of employment of thirteen and a half hours to be taken between 5.30 a.m. and 8.30 p.m. It also provided that employed children should attend school daily for two hours, and required the appointment of four whole-time inspectors.

The Government had builded better than they knew. The boon of the shortened day for children was largely nullified by its connection with the " relay " system ; the school clause was practically inoperative in the majority of cases. But the coming of the inspectors, with their rights of entry at all hours and authority to take information on oath, was the beginning of a new era in the factories. These early inspectors were charged with a tremendous task : fortunately their courage and ability proved equal to it. They cut their way, true pioneers, into the jungle of factory life, and returned from time to time to report their discoveries. With Leonard Horner and his three colleagues factory legislation first began to be a practical force in industry and society ; no public workers of the nineteenth century did more to render a sound social progress possible. Yet they were at first the object of grave suspicion to the operatives. It was taken for granted that Government officials must be the natural allies and confederates of employers, and even supposed that they had been appointed to assist the masters in evading the Act.

On their observations in the factories the future development of industrial regulation was based. But this development was very slow. Between 1833 and 1847 lay thirteen chequered years, in which the hearts of Ashley and the Short Time

Committees grew heavy with frustrated effort.   In 1835, when the introduction of a Ten Hours Bill (under Hindley's management) had been resolved upon, the Government suddenly proposed to amend the existing Act so that the eight-hour day should apply only to children under eleven.   Ashley used the evidence given before the Commission of 1833 with telling effect against Poulett-Thomson's amending Bill, and the second reading was carried by a majority of two only, which led to the dropping of the Bill.   Meanwhile the Inspectors' reports were showing that the schooling of the factory child was a tragic farce and the determination of the age of entry by doctor's rule of thumb—even when honestly applied—an absurdity.[1]

In 1839 Ashley used the occasion of a Factory Bill introduced by the Government (afterwards dropped) to move amendments in favour of shortening hours for young persons, putting silk on the same footing as other textiles and bringing in lace.   His description of what he had seen in the silk and lace mills is only to be paralleled, in these days, by recent reports of British Consuls on the provincial silk filatures of China.   In neither industry was there any limit of age for employment.   In the lace mills, where the hours were from 4 a.m. to 12 p.m., one shift of children were employed to serve two shifts of adults ; as the children's work was intermittent, they lay down on the floor between whiles, in some mills not going home at all for twenty-four hours together.   He was beaten

[1] This difficulty of administration was removed by the passing of the Registration of Births Act in 1837.

on the abortive Bill, but was able to bring forward
his case on silk and lace before the Select Committee appointed, at his instance, to investigate
the working of the 1833 Act. This was the Committee which enquired (among other things) into
the employment of children in the pin-making
trade, to find that the hours of work were 6 a.m.
to 8 p.m., that the children began to work from
five years old and under, and were frequently let
out by their parents to the pin-makers to work off
debts for borrowed money under contracts recognised and enforced by the justices. At fifteen
they were incapable of work, worn out and useless.
Ashley invited the House of Commons to consider
at what cost England was purchasing its trading
pre-eminence, and the Government consented to
bring in two Bills designed to give effect to the
report of his Committee. It fell while both were
in the early stages of their existence. Peel came
into office, with tremendous tasks before him and
no love for factory legislation : it was not till 1843
that he brought in his first Factory Bill, to see it
brought swiftly to shipwreck on the rock of " the
religious difficulty " in education. In 1844 education was left severely alone. The Bill of that year
was chiefly remarkable for the reduction of children's
hours from eight to six and a half (the minimum
age being at the same time lowered from nine to
eight), the regulation of the hours of women for
the first time, the application to silk mills of the
Bill's provisions in full. There was, strangely, little
opposition to the inclusion of women among
protected persons ; all the fury of battle raged

once more about the ten hours day which Ashley attempted to establish indirectly by amendments to certain clauses of the Government measure. Despite the fact that the normal difficulties of his position were increased at this period by recent revelations of the conditions prevailing in the Dorsetshire villages, and not least on his father's estate, he succeeded in carrying the House with him. The House; but not the Government, which, taking its stand on the twelve-hour day, withdrew the Bill and introduced a new one; and when Ashley moved his amendments, threatened resignation if they were carried. Peel made his famous speech on the dangers of leisure for the poor man, and Ashley, though he had the support of Disraeli as well as of the leading Whigs, found his previous narrow majority replaced by crushing defeat. Even so, the unamended Bill encountered heavy weather in the Lords, where Brougham boldly condemned all interference with children's labour and poured ridicule on the provisions for safety, health and cleanliness. Nevertheless, it reached the Statute Book without losing by the way the clause directed to the establishment of a normal day for all protected persons.

In 1845 Ashley returned to the Report of the Children's Employment Commission, which had shown the conditions of child labour in calico printing works to be no whit less inhuman and degrading than in lace mills, and carried his Bill in the face of fierce opposition. He judged it wise—though some of his supporters disagreed with him—not to introduce the Ten Hours Bill that year.

Next year he had to leave the undertaking to Fielden, having resigned his seat on the conscientious ground that he no longer represented his electors on the crucial question of the Corn Laws. He had come to think with Peel, but they had not ; the only honest course was to leave them free to choose another representative. Fielden was beaten by a narrow majority on this occasion ; in 1847, Peel's Government having meanwhile resigned, he carried the cause of Ten Hours to victory. Ashley, who had firmly rejected a suggestion that the reintroduction of the Bill should be postponed till he was again in Parliament, conducted a campaign in its support in Lancashire and Yorkshire. A month later he was back in the House of Commons as member for Bath.

Fielden did not survive his triumph by more than two years, and no one who reads of it can fail to rejoice that it was granted to his singlehearted and unselfish advocacy of a reform by which he risked all that he possessed. At the same time it is permissible to feel more than a little sorry for Ashley. He had not risked his fortune for the factory children, but he had sacrificed his ambition for them, and he was naturally an ambitious man. The sacrifice had been made with open eyes—he knew very well why, when he might legitimately have aspired to a Department, he was offered a place in Prince Albert's household —and yet not without a recurring struggle, for which he reproached himself in secret. Later, he definitely put aside an office which he could have accepted with dignity because his factory work stood in the way. He would not limit his freedom.

His absence from the crucial Session was not rendered easier for him in retrospect by the unhappy Compromise of 1850. The loose wording of the clause of the Act of 1844,[1] which was held to have made intermittent labour of protected persons illegal, was utilised by employers to make the Ten Hours law of none effect. Women and young persons working on the relay system were found by Leonard Horner to have their period of employment extended to fifteen hours, being sent in and out of the factory at the mill-owner's convenience. When appeal was made by a deputation of manufacturers to Sir George Grey, Home Secretary, for an eleven-hour day, he offered to legalise the relay system! Shortly after this, on a test case in the courts, Baron Parke declared the relay system to be already legal, though he admitted that the framers of the Act had probably intended the labour of protected persons to be continuous. Ashley perceived at once the disastrous consequences of this judgment. " Great remedial measure, the Ten Hours Act, nullified. The work to be done all over again ; and I seventeen years older than when I began ! " Unluckily he received two members of the mill-owners' deputation in London, and made some remarks which they misconstrued into acceptance of a sixty-one hours' week. Naturally Oastler, the northern committees and the operatives were up in arms, and Ashley's letters of explanation did little to reassure

[1] This Act was not repealed on the passing of the Act of 1847.

them. He did not go down to the factory districts, and the defence which his friends put up
for him there only intensified the misunderstanding.
A new Committee for the Protection of the Ten
Hours Act came into being, and it was frankly
hostile to Ashley. He had begun by advising the
operatives to stand simply upon their rights under
the Act; now he appeared to be counselling a
compromise with the enemy. Finally, in a letter
to *The Times*, he did, publicly and specifically,
advise the acceptance of the ten-and-a-half hour
day proposed by the Government, in exchange for
abolition of relays and shifts and certain other
advantages, including a normal day ending at
6 p.m.

The result of such a letter was not in doubt, as
Ashley himself clearly foresaw when he wrote it.
The people's confidence in him had been shaken;
under this blow it gave way utterly. The old
Short Time Committees as well as the new Committee for the Protection of the Ten Hours Act
repudiated all idea of a compromise, severed their
connection with Ashley and adopted Lord John
Manners as their representative in Parliament.
Harsh speeches and vehement resolutions, in which
the words "desertion" and "treachery" were
freely used, were reported from Manchester.
When, in the debate on the Bill, Sir George Grey
opposed Ashley's amendment to include children
in the Government measure, and that amendment
was defeated, the cup of Lancashire's wrath was
full, for the exclusion of children from the limited
working day was designed by the Government to

G

ensure that there should be no indirect limitation of the hours of adult men. Once more, at a later stage, Ashley attempted to secure the inclusion of children, and this time he was defeated by one vote only, but it was enough. A little later, a Halifax meeting of delegates, led by Oastler, resolved, " That in the opinion of this meeting Lord Ashley has basely and treacherously betrayed the interests of the factory children." There was much more in the same vein ; Oastler had a fine gift of invective.

The trick to which the Government had meanly resorted in excluding children from the normal day did not remain long in operation. In 1853 Palmerston, who was then Home Secretary, passed a measure including them. But it was not till 1874, under Disraeli, that Cross, by adding half an hour daily to the intervals allowed for meals and rest, gave the textile factory workers the full ten hours' day which they should have enjoyed from 1847 onwards.

Of the Compromise itself there can be but one opinion. Of Ashley's acquiescence in it there may easily be two. Certainly, if he did the right thing on that occasion, he did it in the wrong way ; his letter to *The Times*, published without consultation with the delegates (whom he had promised to consult) was such a display of authoritarianism as self-respecting men could not be expected to accept. But was the substance of his conclusion indeed false ? In view of the Parke judgment and its results, was he not probably wise in believing that the temporary acceptance of a small extension of strictly regulated hours in exchange for licence that was making regulation impossible presented the best available course in the circumstances ? In any case, to expect the defrauded Lancashire operatives to perceive his wisdom was to ask too much.

The North, however, did not show itself permanently unforgiving. When, twenty years later, he went to Bradford for the unveiling of a statue of Oastler, conductor of the campaign of reproach and revilement which he records with more of sorrow than anger in his diary, the vast crowds assembled acclaimed him with enthusiasm as a leader and deliverer. In that hour the two champions, living and dead, so unlike in everything save their devotion to a great cause, were again happily made one.

In striking contrast to the long-drawn-out struggle of the campaign for the Ten Hours Bill, which ended in an imperfect victory for the cause and personal obloquy for the leader to whose thirteen years of devoted labour victory was chiefly due, must be set Ashley's success, comparatively rapid, and all but complete, in his efforts to secure reform in the mines. It cost him thirteen painful years to win for the protected factory workers a ten hours' day, marred in the giving by concessions and omissions which left the door open to interpretation flatly contradictory of his intention; in no more than two after the setting up of the Royal Commission to enquire into the condition of children employed in mines and other industries outside the scope of the

Factory Acts he introduced his Bill founded on the
Commission's Report of April 1842, proposing to
exclude from the coal pits all women and girls,
all boys under thirteen, and all parish apprentices,
and had the satisfaction of seeing it pass into law
in seven weeks.[1]   This signal success came to him,
not after the prolonged struggle for factory legislation was over, but in the midst of it, the result,
as it were, of a flank campaign in his main forward
march.   Indeed, his request for a Royal Commission was in a sense the sequel of his achievement
in obtaining the appointment of a Select Committee to enquire into the working of the Factory
Act of 1833.   Conditions in Parliament and in
the country during 1840, when the promise and
menace of Chartism lit the horizon for half the
nation and brooded darkly over the minds of the
other half, forbade any hope of fresh factory
legislation for the time being; but Ashley, who
had learned from Sadler and Chadwick, as well as
by personal experience, what could be done by
enquiry and report, realised that this period of
enforced Parliamentary inaction might be used to
educate and rouse public opinion to future activity.
Hence his move, first for the Select Committee,
then for the Royal Commission.

It has been suggested that the Whig Government, which gave him the Commission with
unexpected expressions of sympathy, granted the
favour in the spirit of an adult who gives a harm-
less plaything to a troublesome child.   If this

---

[1] After amendment of some of the original provisions by the
House of Lords.

were so, they must have been astonished by the outcome of their indulgence, for the Report of the four sober-minded and practical Commissioners—Tooke, the economist, Dr Southwood Smith, and two Factory Inspectors, of whom one was Leonard Horner—took England by storm and shook the public conscience as few official documents have done in the course of English history. The effect of this Report was no doubt partly due to the fact that by its disclosures the door was opened for the first time upon conditions till then quite unknown to persons of all classes outside the colliery districts. Factories at least carried on their business above ground, and those who worked in them moved among their neighbours in the industrial town and talked freely of the events of their daily life of labour. The colliers were segregated, then as now, in the mining villages, and the story of the sufferings and degradation that were part of the system of their employment in the pits came upon their fellow-countrymen with all the force of novelty : its newness, as well as its horror, stimulated the general imagination. It was in itself horrible enough. Its nearly universal [1] feature was the employment of very young children—seven, six, even five years old—for twelve hours or longer at a time as " trappers " or door-openers controlling the ventilation of the mine in complete darkness and solitude. The youngest children were used for this service ; but it was necessary also to use very little children for

[1] The sole recorded exception is for the North Staffordshire district. There the small children were needed in the Potteries.

the purpose of pushing the small carriages filled with coals along low and narrow passages of which the main gates were only twenty-four to thirty inches high, while in some parts the passages did not exceed a height of eighteen inches, so that even the youngest child had to perform its task "in a bent position." Other children (and women) actually drew the coal carriages on all fours "harnessed like dogs in a go-cart," and yet others stood ankle-deep in water for twelve hours pumping the under-bottoms of the pits. In order to lower the costs of working it was the custom in some districts to substitute small boys for men in the responsible work of letting down and drawing up the cages in which the mine-workers—men, women and children—descended to and returned from their work. That fatal accidents, due to the unfitness of these child "engine-men" for their business, were a frequent occurrence seems to have exercised no check on the practice.

The employment of women and girls was less general, but had been found common in Scotland, South Wales, Cheshire, and some parts of Yorkshire and Lancashire. In Scotland the organisation of work in mines was a good deal more primitive than in England, and the conditions of the workers correspondingly worse. Thus it is reported that the Scottish girls were actually sent down the mine at an earlier age than their brothers; that in some instances girls of six were found carrying half a hundredweight of coal; and that coal was transported from the workings to the pit bottom by gangs of women and children who were used as beasts of burden to carry it in baskets on their backs up steep ladders and along narrow passages. As in the cotton mills, so in the mines the worst sufferers among the child workers were the workhouse apprentices bound for twelve years from the age of eight or nine. Hours varied from a minimum of twelve in most areas to sixteen in Derbyshire, and the Commissioners reported instances in which children working double shifts had remained in the pit for thirty-six hours at a stretch. There was much proved cruelty to the children, and little or no regard for the safety of life or limb either in child or adult. Finally, the conditions under which women and girls worked with and for the miners were shown to outrage the sense of decency as well as of humanity.

A wave of shame and indignation swept over the country on the reading of the Commissioners' tale and flooded the House of Commons itself. When Ashley brought in his Bill he found for once no reason to complain of indifference or lack of sympathy. He had a great case, he presented it greatly, and he carried his audience with him to an unchallenged conclusion. Not a vote was recorded against the Second Reading. Sir James Graham, forgetting or ignoring for the moment his own fixed melancholy conviction that the hardships of the English working population were the outcome of necessary economic law, and therefore incapable of cure or mitigation, accepted Ashley's statement and pledged the Government to " render him every assistance." Lukewarm friends and doubting critics were suddenly changed into admiring sympathisers and supporters; steady opponents rallied to the appeal—Cobden, most consistent and implacable of them, excelling the rest in the generosity of his personal tribute. It must have been a happy hour for Ashley, who had few such hours in his life.

He was soon back in those rough waters whereon the vessel of the social reformer in advance of his time customarily tosses. Before the Bill left the House of Commons it was found necessary to reduce the age of admission to the mines from thirteen to ten, but with the proviso that boys under thirteen should work only on alternate days; when it got into the House of Lords— effecting its appearance there with considerable difficulty, since peer after peer declined to take upon himself the responsibility of introducing it— this proviso was dropped; the employment of parish apprentices under certain limitations was restored; the minimum age of engine-men, which Ashley had fixed at twenty-one, was lowered to fifteen; and the Inspectors authorised in the Bill to report on the state and condition of the mines were, at the instance of Lord Londonderry, de- prived of these powers and permitted only to report on the state and condition of the mine- workers. (The last of these amendments was highly damaging to the Inspectors' usefulness, but eight years elapsed before the false step was re- paired on the initiative of the Government in which Lord John Russell was Prime Minister.) There is no doubt that in the House of Lords, where the influence of the great coal-owners was strong, fear and dislike of the Bill were the ruling sentiments, which the unfriendly attitude of the Duke of Wellington did nothing to modify. But some sense of the strength of feeling behind the measure in the Commons and the country prevented their lordships from throwing it out, and left to Ashley the most unqualified triumph of his career.

No sense of swift or satisfying achievement attaches to the record of his work for Public Health. He did not initiate the Public Health movement. That honour belongs to Chadwick and his medical collaborators on the Poor Law Commission in the sphere of observation and enquiry, and in Parliament to Slaney, who obtained the appointment of the Select Committee to investigate the condition of housing, health, sanitation and water supply. But he was profoundly stirred by the report of the Select Committee in 1840, and in accordance with the rule he had followed in his study of factory conditions, went to see for himself whether the state of things in the slums of Bethnal Green and Whitechapel were indeed as bad as Southwood Smith and other witnesses before the Committee and the Poor Law Commission had painted them. Southwood Smith had not minced his words in giving evidence. He declared that all the suffering he described was preventible. The effect on the sufferers was the same as if twenty or thirty thousand of them were annually taken out of their homes and put to death—the only difference being that they were left in them to die. Ashley, accompanying this medical observer over his field of observation,

found that " no pen or paint-brush could describe
the thing as it is. One whiff of Cowyard, Blue
Anchor or Bakers' Court, outweighs ten pages of
letterpress." And he blesses God that he forms
no part of the existing Government (whose return,
as a staunch Conservative, he had helped to secure)
which had just refused to adopt the two Bills
introduced by Lord Normanby, Home Secretary
in the fallen Whig Government, to deal with
housing, ventilation and drainage. These Bills
would have given Town Councils power to take
land by compulsion for the achievement of their
object, and actually went so far as to prohibit the
building of back-to-back houses.[1] Ashley, at Normanby's request, tried to keep them alive in the
Commons, and though, as a private member, he
could not force Peel to introduce legislation, his
action helped to emphasise the profound effect
produced by the Poor Law Commission Report of
1842, and to ensure the appointment of the Commission on the Health of Towns. That Commission, under Chadwick's influence, reported in
1844 in such terms that legislation appeared
inevitable, for, in the absence of any general
sanitary authority in towns and the extraordinary
difficulties, legal and financial, to be surmounted
by any municipality desirous of improving the
conditions of its population or controlling in any
way the development of its own area, it was clear
that nothing short of national action would avail

[1] This reform was not achieved till 1909. So slowly does
the public conscience, even when allied with scientific knowledge,
get the upper hand of vested interests !

in the face of existing dangers and abuses. Unfortunately the great struggle over the Corn Laws intervened to create delay, and it was not till four years later that the country obtained the first Public Health Act.

As the admission of a principle the Act was invaluable ; as a scheme of reform it was inadequate ; as a piece of administrative legislation it was clumsy and ill-adapted to its ends. The work of the Central Authority, a General Board of Health composed of three (subsequently increased to four) Commissioners, was inquisitorial rather than constructive, being so planned as to irritate local authorities instead of inviting them to friendly co-operation. That it was independent of Parliament exposed it to suspicion and put an additional weapon into the hand of the representatives of the landlords, the monopolist vested interests and the convinced disciples of *laissez-faire*, who formed a strange and heterogeneous confederation against it. At the same time its powers were to a large extent illusory, for a reactionary authority was free to defy it. That Chadwick and Ashley should be two of the first Commissioners appointed can excite no surprise, but they were not men well fitted by temperament to make the working of such a statute as the Public Health Act of 1848 successful in the circumstances of the time. Chadwick was first and foremost a bureaucrat, and although Ashley was capable of working wholeheartedly with men to whose general opinions and methods he was opposed so long as they and he were engaged in the same crusade—witness his

generous appreciation of Oastler—he had no apti-
tude for peaceful persuasion of recalcitrant town
councillors callously indifferent to the sufferings of
the poor. It is not surprising that under such
guidance the Board made serious mistakes, and
that the unpopularity which led to its extinction
in 1854 was not altogether undeserved. Nevertheless it would be a mistake to dismiss its work
slightingly or to undervalue Ashley's share in it.
His Housing Bills of 1851, for all their short-
comings, showed a practical grasp of certain
aspects of the housing problem remarkable at that
date, and it is to be noted that he did not
even then overlook the hardships which re-building
schemes would impose on dispossessed tenants and
the need for providing against them. Nor must
the action of the Board in its dealings with the
water supply and drainage of London be forgotten.
To Ashley, who always threw himself heart and
mind into every task he undertook, his administrative duties at the Board proved an occasion of
new knowledge, of which he made fine use a year
or two after the Board itself, to his grief and
resentment, had been put to death. Few people
probably remember at this date that it was to
Shaftesbury (he had succeeded his father in 1851)
we owe the memorable Sanitary Commission which,
in the judgment of Florence Nightingale, saved the
British Army of the Crimea of 1855.

Shaftesbury's official part in public health work
was comparatively brief ; not so his labours as a
Commissioner in Lunacy, which ended only with
his life and covered a period of fifty-seven years.

For over half a century he was Chairman of the Board, and during his term of service saw the fundamental change—distressingly slow, but always in one direction—from cruelty to humanity and from ignorance to scientific method in the treatment of the insane, the gradual building of safeguards against illegal, improper and unnecessary certification, the creation of the public asylum and the steady development of a system of inspection extended to all establishments in which lunatics could be received. Of all his undertakings there was none which called for more personal devotion, none in which he needed more acutely the support of his religious faith. During his first twenty years as a Commissioner he regularly visited the asylums, and even after that date, when—as he told the Select Committee of 1877—he was able to leave statutory visiting to the professional members of his Commission, he continued to visit in special cases. Throughout the earlier period his investigations brought him continually into contact with scenes and conditions horrible and repulsive beyond present-day imagination ; his work at the Board was heavy and continuous ; he had to fight unceasingly for seventeen years to obtain the reforming Act of 1845 ; and the later years of his long administration were repeatedly disturbed by violent attacks on the Commissioners and on himself personally in Parliament and in the Press. No doubt he tended, as he grew old, to rest overmuch on past achievement, and his passionate resistance to the proposal that every " order for admission " must be signed by a magistrate, on the ground that it would prevent early treatment, seems to us strangely ill-founded. But he was not alone in this view, which was shared by many specially qualified medical men ; and it was perhaps only natural that one to whose memory the conditions of 1828 were still vividly present should tend to dwell, in 1885, rather on the reform that had been wrought than on the need for further improvement.

No student of Shaftesbury's activities will overlook his efforts to liberate the Climbing Boys. It was in 1840 that he espoused the cause of the child chimney-sweep, who had not altogether lacked indignant champions since Jonas Hanway made his miserable lot known to the England of 1773. Blake and Dickens were among them ; even the unreformed House of Commons passed several Bills to prohibit the use of climbing boys, which were steadily rejected by the Lords. The hideous exploitation of small ill-used children went on unchecked till Lord Normanby, supported by Ashley in the Lower House, succeeded in carrying to the Statute Book an Act which forbade the climbing of chimneys by any person under twenty-one. But it was one thing to pass the Measure, another to enforce it. Observed in London and some provincial cities, it was ignored in industrial areas and in country houses, and magistrates took no steps to punish breaches of the Act. Now and then a peculiarly terrible case of suffocation in a chimney, or of such brutal treatment as brought the Manchester sweep, Gordon, to trial for man-slaughter in 1847, became known, but public

opinion remained apathetic. The Climbing Boys'
Society, with Shaftesbury as President, did what it
could by collecting evidence of deaths and ill-
treatment, and of buying and selling of children,
and by taking prosecutions. Repeated attempts at
further legislation failed in one House or the other ;
revelations of the most horrifying nature before
Select Committees left legislators still willing to
leave reform " entirely to the moral feelings of
perhaps the most moral people on the face of the
earth." A note of something like despair creeps
into Shaftesbury's journal. The earlier " Anxious,
very anxious about my sweeps " becomes : " Again
I must bow to this mysterious Providence that
leaves these outcasts to their horrible destiny and
nullifies, apparently at least, all our efforts to
ensure them in soul and body."

Not till 1875 did the old system receive its
death-blow. In that year—moved by two cruel
deaths on which he had founded a fresh appeal for
public action through *The Times*—Shaftesbury
brought in yet another Chimney-sweeps' Bill. It
provided that no chimney-sweep should carry on
his trade without an annual licence from the police,
who were charged with enforcement of the existing
Acts ; for breach of those Acts the sweep might
be deprived of his licence. The Bill passed easily
—and the tragic figure of the climbing boy vanished
from the social scene.

Shaftesbury's initiative in bringing about the
break-up of the iniquitous gang system by which a
new kind of child slavery had been introduced into
the agricultural districts must pass here with bare

mention. Of his concern for the young offender, and that mass of philanthropic work which—with the beloved Ragged Schools holding first place—lay so near his heart, it is not possible to write at all. Probably, as Mr and Mrs Hammond argue in their admirable *Life*, he undertook too much, and not only wasted strength but weakened judgment by the diversity of his interests; a better sense of proportion would have made him doubly effective along the main lines of his effort. Nevertheless, his inability to leave well alone, especially where individual sinners and sufferers were concerned, had its uses: it helped him to bring to his central work of re-humanising industry at the point where it tended to become devilish, that work which has made him a great historical figure, the profound respect for human life and the passionate belief in human value by which he awakened the paralysed public conscience of nineteenth-century England.

But he did more than this. An awakened public conscience, if it is not to spend itself in futile emotion, must find a channel of expression. Shaftesbury taught it to speak with the voice of law; and the lesson which he gave to his own generation now resounds throughout the civilised world.

Painting by
A. Scheffer

National Portrait
Gallery

CHARLES DICKENS

CHARLES DICKENS (1812-70)

By A. J. CARLYLE, M.A., D.Litt.

CHARLES DICKENS

IT is not always quite realised that Dickens is not an English artist merely ; he is an artist who has had a greater effect in Europe than any other English artist since Byron and Scott. We can still find the traces of the enormous influence which Dickens has exercised from the Pacific States of America to the novels and tales of Russia. There are few countries in Europe where we cannot trace the effects of his immense human sense of love—in France, in Germany, in Russia, and probably I should add Italy and Scandinavia—everywhere in literature, and, what is probably no less important, in the actual sense of human life, we can find something of the influence which Dickens has exercised. It may be doubted indeed whether any man since St Francis of Assisi has had the same effect in Europe in quickening the sense of sympathy and of the kindly feelings of men for each other.

What is not always understood is that this was in a very real sense a revival of Christianity. How far Dickens himself was completely conscious of this or not is another matter, but the foundation of Dickens' sense of life is the same as that which is characteristic of Christianity in its earliest and also in its best forms. There are some people who complain that in these days we are too humane, and it is possible that our humanity sometimes becomes sentimental, but the complaint is really short-sighted and foolish, for there are very few things which do more definitely distinguish the temper of Christianity from that of the ancient world than this very humanity. The civilisation of the ancients, whether Greek or Roman, had splendid characteristics. It was just and wise ; the Greek civilisation especially had the highest and finest sense of beauty, but the Hellenic world, as well as the Roman world, was hard, and it was only in the centuries which preceded the coming of Christianity into the world that the humane temper began to appear.

This humane temper had, if we will recognise it, its philosophical and logical foundation, for it is probably true to say that what lies behind the growth of this humane temper is the gradual development, even among the abstract thinkers and philosophers of the centuries immediately preceding the Christian era, of the recognition of what we call personality. It is a noticeable thing that the great Greek thinkers, with all their greatness, had a very imperfect sense of the significance of individuality. This conception grew up in the centuries immediately preceding the birth of Christ, and found its appropriate form in the conception of human equality. While the great Greek thinkers of the fourth and fifth centuries before Christ, looking out on the world, had found a spectacle of inequality, of rational men who were masters and irrational men who were slaves, the world, even before the coming of Christ, had discovered that men were equals, that is, that as human beings they had all something alike, they were of equal value, of equal spiritual and moral quality.

This was the doctrine that was taken up into Christianity, and it is one of its most essential features, for, to Christ and to those who best understood him, men were all the children of one Father, capable of a life of communion with Him, and were all, therefore, to each other brothers and friends. It is no doubt true that, in the course of the Christian centuries, much of this was forgotten, and it is true that, if we consider the temper and characteristics of the Middle Ages, and recognise some great exceptions like St Francis, the mediæval world was again harsh and hard, like the Greek; great, powerful, and often wise, but lacking in humanity, wanting in a sense of the infinite value of little things. From this confusion the world had begun to awake some hundred years before Dickens was born. It had begun to awake, for there is much in what is called the sensibility of the eighteenth century which really represents the revival of this humane sense. Whether men had learnt it from great Christians, like Fénelon, or from great men who conceived themselves to be the enemies of the Christian religion, like Voltaire, does not greatly matter. Men were learning it, and it is in the humane movements of the latter part of the eighteenth century and the early part of the nineteenth century, in the demand for the abolition of slavery and in the gradual development of the Factory Acts, that we can see the signs of this.

While it is true, therefore, that the world into

which Charles Dickens was born was a world which was learning humanity, it is also true that the world into which he was born was not only hard but squalid. The circumstances of his birth and his early life made him familiar with the cruel and ugly aspects of human life in England, and it is the remarkable thing about Charles Dickens that this experience did not make him hard, but made him kindly and sympathetic. For this is the first and the greatest characteristic of Dickens as a man, that his heart was full of sympathy with human nature, and infinitely pitiful towards human suffering. He was not, indeed, the first to whom the little child was dear. Blake and Wordsworth had preceded him, but yet it may be doubted whether Blake or Wordsworth as much as Dickens created the modern sense of compassion and pity as well as of love for all children.

There are some purists of literature who will always be found to object to Dickens that, in some of his novels at least, he is not only creating a work of art but preaching a sermon, and yet who is there who will really think that it was not well done ? Dickens looked about him and saw the miserable conditions of childhood in the workhouses of England in the early nineteenth century, and he wrote *Oliver Twist*. The reform in the treatment of children under Poor Law has indeed come slowly ; it is not so long since we might all have been familiar with the condition of children in the mixed workhouses. But if the reform has come slowly, it has come steadily, and we may well hope that the twentieth century will see the end of a bad system, and if it is ended it will be due very largely to the power as well as the pathos with which Dickens described the life of little Oliver. He looked out again on the world as he knew it, and he saw the disgraceful treatment of children in many of the schools of his day, and he wrote *Nicholas Nickleby*, and described the miserable lot of poor Smike in Dotheboys' Hall. It is difficult to know whether we are more affected by the satirical humour of the picture of Mr Squeers and his school, or by the pathetic story of poor Smike. But indeed always and everywhere the love and pity for little children under every condition and of every class is shown in his novels. Whether it is little Nell or little Paul Dombey, he compelled men to see and to understand and feel with the child.

But it was not only children whom Dickens loved and for whom he had sympathy. All unhappy creatures, all the pathetic figures of human life, moved him to sympathy and even to tears. Whether it is Nancy or little Em, or the unhappy woman of every class and degree, we may blame, but Dickens pities. And so again with the poor, with the prisoners. The conditions of the debtors' prisons is happily to us an old story, belonging to old and far-off things, but there can be little doubt that it was Dickens' description of the conditions under which men and women lived in the Marshalsea and in other debtors' prisons which contributed more than any other one cause to the abolition of a dreadful state of things. The truth is that over all human life there plays the loving and tender fancy, the immense compassion and pity of Charles Dickens. Dickens may be, and probably is, often over-sentimental, but there are few people still who can read or hear read the story of the *Christmas Carol* without being moved to sympathy and love of human nature.

It is, of course, quite true that all this gracious humanity of Dickens would have only had half its effect if in all his work there was not to be found his riotous and penetrating but kindly humour. No doubt there were some things, perhaps even some persons, whom Dickens hated—the hypocrite, the pretentious, the cruel—to such persons he may even sometimes be himself a little cruel, but in the main how genial is the laughter, for he sees the world, not only as pitiful, but as astonishingly gay and laughable. Since Shakespeare it is probably true to say that there has been no artist who has had so real an understanding of the great-hearted laughter of human life. Sam Weller and his old father may not be on the same level as Falstaff, but they are probably the only figures in English literature who come somewhere near Falstaff, and it may perhaps be said that Dickens even does some things in this way which Shakespeare himself has not done. For to Dickens there are no commonplace or uninteresting persons in life. To him the very fact of humanity lends an interest, and he gives us in figures, which at first glance may seem the most ordinary and the most commonplace, the elements of the most genial humanity. Who would think that the absurd little fat man of the early part of Pickwick would

become the kindly, honest and just man of the
later part ?

Or, again, if we want other examples, we need
only think of Mr Micawber, laughable, stupid and
yet so very human, or of the Marchioness, the little
maid of all work, the " slavey," slatternly, untidy,
draggle-tailed, and yet Dickens compels us to see, to
smile, but also to understand. Dickens is indeed
not isolated; as we said before, he comes out of
the sensibility of the eighteenth century, he has
his predecessors in England, above all Sterne, he
belongs indeed to the illustrious company of Sterne's
pupils, like Jean Paul Richter in Germany, but like
Richter, he has shaken off much of the maudlin
sensibility, and all of the stupid lubricity of Sterne's
work. We cannot say that his pathos and humour
are greater than Sterne's at his best, but his range
is larger, his humour is heartier, more robust, there
is more laughter and less snigger. And he has also
illustrious successors. Not to mention Daudet in
France, it is pretty certain that he has had much
to do with the farcical and sentimental humour of
American literature from Bret Harte to O'Henry ;
and, partly at least through the Americans, how
much there is in Kipling of the tradition of Dickens ;
for I think he would have recognised the little
"friend of all the world " and the old Buddhist
monk, as belonging to his house, and he would have
understood Mulvaney and Ortheris and Learoyd.

We hardly know indeed how much we owe to
this immense human genius of Dickens. It was
not altogether unreasonable when Tolstoy, in his
little book on art, spoke of him as the greatest

of modern artists. For though he may have a thousand faults—indeed, it is easy for any fool to discover the faults in Dickens—he has qualities which are almost incomparable, and the greatest of all these qualities is that he is so human. The criticism of the great Tolstoy explains how even he himself followed the example which Dickens had set, in many of his most gracious tales. And it is probably not exaggerating if we say that the great if sombre genius of Dostoievsky represents, in its sheer sense of the value of human nature, much that is derived from Charles Dickens, as again it is not too much to say that much of what is most moving and most significant in Victor Hugo's *Les Miserables* represents the tradition of Dickens.

And in all this we should not let ourselves be mistaken. Dickens was, consciously or unconsciously, doing much to recreate the Christian conception of human life. For surely it is the very characteristic of the Gospels that there is no one too little or insignificant to belong to the great household of God, and in his own way and in his own terms Charles Dickens was saying something of the same kind.

FLORENCE NIGHTINGALE

FLORENCE NIGHTINGALE
(1820–1910)
By MARY SCHARLIEB, D.B.E., M.D., M.S., J.P.

FLORENCE NIGHTINGALE

I THINK we may venture to say that Florence Nightingale was not only a remarkable woman, remarkable in her own day and generation, but even that she is one of the outstanding personalities of all time. If ever there was an individual with a Vocation, it was Florence Nightingale, and if there be such a thing as whole-hearted response, persistently and faithfully carried out from early life to extreme old age, such a response to God's Call was made by Florence Nightingale. She herself said in an autobiographical fragment: "God called her to His service" in February 1837. She was then seventeen years of age, and her devotion to the service of God and man endured until she passed into the land of higher service at the age of ninety.

At first, indeed, the call to service was not definite. She was bidden to go and work in the vineyard, but the exact nature of the work required of her had not, as yet, become apparent to her consciousness. From the very beginning she knew that her call was to the active life, that she was to be cumbered with much serving, and, very clearly, the study of her life reveals that never at any time did she feel that for her the path of duty led to the cloister, or indeed to the life of subordination of any kind. At first, as a very young girl, the daughter of a wealthy man, her attempt at response to the Call consisted in visiting her poorer neighbours and in ministering to their wants. As she herself says, she "worked very hard among the poor people under a strong feeling of religion." It is likely that the early uncertainty would have cleared more quickly had she remained at home, but it suited her father's plans that the whole family should go abroad, and for a couple of years Mr and Mrs Nightingale and their two young daughters, Parthenope and Florence, travelled in France, Italy and Switzerland. Mr Nightingale had himself superintended his daughters' education, and their studies included Greek, Latin and many subjects that were quite unusual for women in those days.

The conditions of the European world at the time, and the nature of the society which surrounded the Nightingales abroad, were well calculated to develop the eager young woman who was so deeply interested in her fellow-creatures. Sir Edward Cook, whose two big volumes tell the story of Florence Nightingale's life and work, has painted a most interesting picture of the Court balls, the music, and the political agitation which made up the stimulating diet on which her young mind was fed. Sir Edward records that the greatest pleasure enjoyed by Florence during these crowded days was the Italian Opera, and that for some time after her return home, she was, as she said herself, "music-mad." Among the other great assets of these wonderful months was the formation of her lifelong friendship with Miss Mary Clarke, after-

wards Madame Mohl. She introduced the Nightingales into the most exclusive and literary society
in Paris. Among the many remarkable people with
whom Florence thus became acquainted was the
celebrated Madame Récamier. It is interesting
to note how the instrument intended by God for
very special work was formed by Him from the
days of childhood, and how it was sharpened, set,
and polished by Him, so as to be worthy of His use
and to be efficient in the task assigned to it.

Florence's response to the call might have been
endangered by the social successes of this Grand
Tour, and perhaps more by the subsequent winters
spent in Rome and in Egypt, and still more, it
might have been misinterpreted and misdirected,
had she yielded to a somewhat later temptation to
the married life. She had many and suitable offers.
Once, at any rate, the admiring love that she had
inspired was, to some extent, returned by her, and
she seems to have hesitated before definitely re-
nouncing what she herself regarded as the better
life for women. In her own case, feeling that God
had called her to some special work for Him and for
mankind, she doubted whether marriage, with the
very onerous duties which it entails, would be compatible with the development of her best and
strongest powers. Sir Edward Cook quotes the
following passage from her diary in the year 1850:
" I am thirty, the age at which Christ began His
mission. Now, no more childish things, no more
vain things, no more love, no more marriage.
Now, Lord, let me only think of Thy Will." All
this entailed a true sacrifice, and a sacrifice all the

greater because, even at the age of thirty, the exact nature of the work required had not been disclosed to her. But by now she at any rate knew that she was appointed to open out some better life for her many sisters for whom the joys of wifehood and motherhood were unattainable. For herself a prevision that nursing was her appointed lot had grown with her growth and strengthened with her strength, and yet she could do nothing in the direction of training. It is true that her father was a wealthy man, and that she was tenderly beloved by him, by her mother and her only sister, but she had no money of her own, and none of her family circle sympathised in the very smallest degree with her aspirations. Mrs Nightingale hoped that both her daughters would marry, be good wives and mothers, happy, as she herself was happy, in the conscientious discharge of domestic and social duties. Florence felt very deeply that the life of duty, as it presented itself to her, inevitably cut across her parents' aspirations for her and across her sister's sympathies. She tried hard, she tried repeatedly, but she tried in vain, to put away her ideal from her. So stern was the conflict that by the age of thirty-one she was convinced that nothing was desirable for her but death. The home-life that to all around her appeared so desirable was to her not only a weariness but a cross, and she felt that if suitable opportunities of service could not be given her, she must take them for herself. By this time she was fully determined that she would be a nurse, and minister to the physical necessities of the sick and suffering. But nothing but the best was good enough for her.

Like David, she could not offer to the Lord her God that which had cost her nothing, and she recognised that in addition to the heavy moral cost of her offering, she must add that of delay in the accomplishment of her purpose in order that the treasure she proposed to dedicate should be the best of its kind.

She had heard of the wonderful Institution for Deaconesses at Kaiserswerth, near Düsseldorf. This had been founded in the early eighteen hundreds by Pastor Theodor Fliedner. He and his wife had begun their work of a " Prison Association " by receiving into their summer house one discharged prisoner ! This was followed after a brief interval by a tiny Infant School and a Hospital wherein they hoped to train nurses. From this mustard seed had sprung a goodly tree, and by the time that Florence Nightingale was able to take advantage of training there, Kaiserswerth had a Hospital of 100 beds, an Infant School, an Orphan Asylum, a Normal School, a Penitentiary and 116 Deaconesses, 67 resident there and the rest scattered throughout Germany. To this extraordinary union of many good works came Florence Nightingale, with her eager soul, her orderly mind, and her determination that her preparation for future work should be of the best. Of Kaiserswerth she said herself that " nursing there was *nil*. The hygiene horrible. The Hospital was certainly the worst part of Kaiserswerth. I took all the training there was to be had— there was none to be had in England—but Kaiserswerth was far from having trained me. On the other hand, the tone was excellent, admirable."

I

Florence stayed at Kaiserswerth for three months and returned home, where she was to make herself useful in domestic nursing for the time being. A different temptation to a bypath now occurred, this time in the form of literature. She wrote a novel, of which no trace remains, and a book on religion, *Suggestions for Thought*, the first volume of which was dedicated to the artisans of England. As she quaintly says, she thought of giving " a new religion to the tailors." It was certainly fortunate for the due accomplishment of Miss Nightingale's life-work that these early literary ventures proved to be merely the preparation for the truly admirable books she published in later years, such as, *Notes on Nursing*, *Notes on Hospitals*, *Notes on Lying-in Institutions*.

The interval between Florence Nightingale's return from Kaiserswerth and the outbreak of the Crimean War was amply filled by home nursing, by writing, by cheering intercourse with her " Aunt Mai," and the formation of various friendships which were destined to bear excellent fruit in the future. Aunt Mai proved a most useful mediator between the parents who so greatly desired social success for her and the daughter who believed that she had found a more excellent way for herself. Very early in 1853 the uncompromising young lady left London with her cousin, Miss Bonham Carter, for Paris. They stayed with Monsieur and Madame Mohl and partook of the gaieties of the French Capital. Florence intended to have settled down with the Sisters of Charity, but she was recalled home by her grandmother's illness and death. She had, however, had time enough to see something of surgery as interpreted by great Paris surgeons.

The next move was to be Superintendent of an Establishment for Gentlewomen during Illness in Harley Street. In this position no doubt our enthusiast learnt practically what it meant to work under a Committee, for in one of her letters to Madame Mohl she wrote : " From Committees, Charity and Schism—from the Church of England and all other deadly sins—from philanthropy and all deceits of the devil, Good Lord, deliver us ! " The experience gained at such cost to temper and to feeling was exceedingly useful, and Florence Nightingale had in her the grit that was necessary to carry her through the many difficulties in future life, of which her work in Harley Street was but the faintest foreshadow.

In August 1854 there was a proposal that she should be Superintendent of Nurses at King's College Hospital. However, before this offer could be accepted, the Crimean War burst on the Nation, and its first note was that of disaster. The battle of the Alma was fought on 20th September 1854, and although it was a great occasion of national pride, it was also one for national mourning and for national indignation. The failure to provide for the sick and wounded had caused so heavy a toll to be taken of valuable lives. The *Times* set afoot an appeal for funds and for personal service. Among the many who took the appeal strongly to heart were Lady Maria Forester, who was anxious to give money to send out trained nurses, Mr Sidney Herbert, the Secretary at War, and Florence Nightingale, who had waited thirty-four years for her opportunity for service, flung herself into the breach with a God-inspired enthusiasm which sufficed to carry her through all difficulties and all disaster to the completion of her work.

The Alma was fought on the 20th September, and on the 21st of October, the anniversary of Trafalgar as one must remember, Florence Nightingale and thirty-eight nurses left London, making halts in Paris and Marseilles, and arriving at Scutari in due course.

The whole thing was an experiment which might fail, therefore it was clearly understood that additional nurses should be sent out only if and when the Lady-in-Chief asked for them, but it may as well be noted at once that after a short lapse of time other nurses did follow to the Crimea, led by Miss Stanley, an old friend of Florence Nightingale's. She was far from pleased at their arrival, for she felt that her position was already sufficiently difficult between indignant military and medical authorities on the one hand and the undisciplined nurses on the other. Good and self-sacrificing as they were, the sudden arrival of the unasked-for contingent placed the chief lady in an extremely difficult and trying position.

Very fortunately for Miss Nightingale and for her work, Mr Sidney Herbert, the Minister at War, was as anxious for its success as she was herself. He believed that she was the only person who could make the Nursing Mission successful, and he doubted whether it were possible even for her. To add to Miss Nightingale's difficulties, there were certain religious and social problems which required the most anxious care and management. Some authorities objected to the presence of the Roman Catholics, others to that of the Nonconformists, nay, even the distinction between the two schools of thought within the Church of England gave rise to an amusing incident. Sir Edward tells us that " one of Miss Stanley's ladies was accused by a certain Chaplain of circulating improper books in the wards. Particulars were asked, and it was found that the offending book was Keble's *Christian Year* ! "

It also appears that a question was asked at the War Office as to why there were no Presbyterians amongst the nurses. Miss Nightingale wrote in reply : " I object to the principle of sending out any one *quâ* sectarian, not *quâ* nurse. . . . Let six trained nurses be sent out if you think fit, of whom let two-thirds be Presbyterians. . . . Above fourteen stone we will not have, the provision of bedsteads is not strong enough."

The hospitals at Scutari under Miss Nightingale's charge were four. They were uncomfortable and crowded. The Battle of the Alma had shown how terrible was the pressure on beds and on attention. Miss Nightingale and a friend, Mrs Bracebridge, normally slept in one small room, Mr Bracebridge and the courier in another. But the space allotted to the whole Nursing contingent was only equal to that occupied by the Commandant. The position would have been intolerable had not Miss Nightingale taken a separate house in Scutari, to which nurses sick with fever could be removed. Not only space and beds were lacking, but the commonest necessities and utensils did not exist. Needless to say that there were no so-called hospital comforts, such as arrowroot, meat essences, wine and brandy. Stores, no doubt, did exist, but they were so packed, so stored in vessels under military requirements, and so landed, or not landed, that they were not available. Here what was necessary was the clear head and enormous courage that had been bestowed upon Florence Nightingale, and she used them well.

Among the many things that Florence Nightingale did not find at Scutari were the absolutely necessary utensils for cleanliness of person, quarters and linen. There were no basins, towels, brooms, or soap, no scrubbing brushes. Patients' clothes were not washed, six shirts only in one month. There was no hot water. Everything was washed in cold. Not unnaturally the vermin was not destroyed. Miss Nightingale took a house outside the Hospital, supplied it with boilers and other utensils and employed soldiers' wives to do the washing. There were no facilities for extra diet, but although Miss Nightingale could not always follow the exact regulations for the supply of food and other necessaries, she was very careful to supply nothing from her own Stores except in answer to the doctors' requisitions and then only when Government supplies failed. As to the cooking of the food, an enormous improvement was made in 1855, when Alexis Soyer, the ex-chef of the Reform Club, arrived and did excellent work in superintending the cooking for the sick and wounded.

A quotation from a letter of Lord Raglan's,

reprinted in one of Sir Edward Cook's fascinating volumes, showed what she did with these gifts.

"The popular voice thought of her only or mainly as the gentle nurse. That, too, she was; and to her self-devotion applying her woman's insight to a new sphere, a portion of her fame must ever be ascribed. But when men who knew all the facts spoke of her commanding genius, it was rather of her work as an administrator that they were thinking. They could scarcely realise, without personally seeing it, the heartfelt gratitude of the soldiers or the amount of misery which had been relieved by Miss Nightingale and her nurses, and, he added, it was impossible to do justice to the kindness of heart, or to the clever judgment, the ready intelligence, and the experience displayed by the distinguished lady to whom this difficult mission had been entrusted. . . . She did the work in three ways. She applied an expert's touch and a woman's insight to a Hospital hitherto managed exclusively by men. She boldly assumed responsibility, and did things herself which she could find no one else ready to do. And, thirdly, she was instant and persistent in suggestion, exhortation, reproaches addressed to the authorities at home."

It is gratifying to know that throughout all her difficulties and annoyances, Lord Raglan stood by her and supported her by his great position and influence.

Minor difficulties in the way of this devoted woman are illustrated by the remarks of a nurse quoted by Miss Nightingale in a letter to her friend, Dr Bowman : " I came out, Ma'am, prepared to submit to everything, to be put upon in every way. But there are some things, Ma'am, one can't submit to. There is the Caps, Ma'am, that suits one face, and some that suits another. And if I'd known, Ma'am, about the Caps, great as was my desire to come out to nurse at Scutari, I wouldn't have come, Ma'am."

Further on in the same letter, Miss Nightingale tells us, " We have our quarters in one tower of the barrack, and all this fresh influx of patients has been laid down between us and the main guard in the two corridors with a line of beds down each side, just room for one person to pass between, and four wards. In the midst of this appalling horror (we are steeped up to our necks in blood) there is good, and I can truly say, like St Peter, it is good for us to be here—though I doubt if St Peter had been here, he would have said so."

Among other gifts enjoyed by Florence Nightin-ingale was the power of delegating her work. To be, as she put it, Matron of the Hospitals and Mistress of the Barracks was a more than sufficiently heavy burden for any one individual, and she did very wisely in assigning to her friend, Mrs Brace-bridge, the care of the women camp followers, and to Lady Alicia Blackwood the care of the Lying-in Hospital.

Naturally enough, Florence Nightingale's extraordinary degree of initiative power, her fearlessness, and perhaps even more the uncanny way in which she managed to exercise these powers with the least possible contravention of rules, regulations, and even of medical etiquette made her both warm friends and bitter enemies. It was quite evident that the supplies secured by her, the reforms introduced by her and the enormous increase of comfort and well-being among the troops which had been secured by her, must have been still more readily within the grasp of ordinary officers, both military and medical, but probably there is nothing that more effectually arouses indignation and resentment than the sight of another person doing one's own job and doing it far better than one ever did it one's self. Mercifully Florence Nightingale was endowed not only with a clear head and a warm heart but also with that ever blessed sense of humour, and that sort of temper which is compatible with a well-directed blow to-day, and the power of seeing the other fellow's point of view, which by no means forbids the friendship of to-morrow.

Throughout all her difficulties, disappointments, and even failures, for indeed she was not superhuman, Miss Nightingale could rely not only on the forces of her own character, but also on the steadfast support and ready sympathy of such men as Sidney Herbert, Minister at War, and Mr Bracebridge, than whom no one was more competent to judge of her work. Another powerful asset was the great appreciation shown by Her Majesty, Queen Victoria, and by her Court. Indeed, the Queen, in writing to Mrs Herbert, begged her to let Miss Nightingale know of her sympathy. In the Queen's own words : " Let Mrs Herbert also know that I wish Miss Nightingale and the ladies would tell these poor noble and wounded and sick men that *no one* takes a warmer interest and feels *more* for their sufferings, and admires their courage and heroism *more* than their Queen. Day and night she thinks of her beloved troops. . . . So does the Prince. . . . I know that our sympathy is much valued by these noble fellows." About the same

time Her Majesty forwarded a substantial proof
of her sympathy in gifts of comforts for the
wounded and kind little remembrances to Miss
Nightingale's nurses.

It appears, however, that even the strong influence
of Ministers and the sympathy of a Queen did not
avail to overcome the *vis inertiæ* and the lack of
order which had so interfered with the welfare of
the troops in the field. To remedy this, a special
sanitary commission was necessary. Three very
suitable men, Dr Sutherland, Dr Gavin, and Mr
Rawlinson, were sent out armed with full executive
powers, and from that moment the situation was
redeemed. As Miss Nightingale said to Lord
Shaftesbury, "This Commission saved the British
Army." It is worthy of note that the friendship then
formed with Dr Sutherland and Mr Rawlinson was
lifelong. Dr Gavin, however, died in the Crimea.

In the little space of this article it is not possible
to tell the full story, nor even to mention with any
detail the manifold reforms instituted by Miss
Nightingale, and in most instances carried by her
to a successful issue. She secured the formation of
a medical school at Scutari. She induced the
authorities to arrange for the men to send home
portions of their pay for the support of their families.
The records of the past, however, show quite
clearly that the side of Florence Nightingale's
character and life which was best understood by the
public at home was that of the " ministering angel."
As Sir Edward Cook reports : " The men idolised
her. They kissed her shadow, and they saluted her
as she passed down their wounded ranks. ' If the

Queen came for to die,' said a soldier, who lost a
leg at the Alma, ' they ought to make her Queen,
and I think they would.' . . . ' She was wonderful,' said one, ' at cheering up any one who was a
bit low.' ' She was all full of life and fun,' said
another, ' when she talked to us, especially if a man
was a bit downhearted.' Who can tell what
comfort was brought by the sound of a woman's
gentle voice, the touch of a woman's gentle hand, to
many a poor fellow racked by fever or smarting
from sores ? And who can say how often her
presence may have been as a cup of strength in some
great agony ? . . . If the soldiers were told that
the roof had opened and that she had gone up
palpably to Heaven, they would not have been in the
least surprised. They quite believed she was in
several places at once."

It is not to be supposed that all that was attempted
and all that was won by this noble woman was done
without cost to herself. She never faltered nor
left her post ; strenuous days were followed by long
hours of writing and short hours of sleep in the
night. She felt, with the keenness that only knowledge could give, grief for the unnecessary sufferings
and mortality of the troops. She saw her colleagues
and her nurses die around her. She must have
felt that she held her life on the shortest possible
tenure, and once, indeed, her health broke down
badly, when she was on a visit to the Crimea, where
there were many hospitals she wanted to inspect.

She found the conditions in the Crimea even
worse than they had been at Scutari. In May
1855 Miss Nightingale wrote : " Fancy working five

nights out of seven in the trenches! Fancy being thirty-six hours in them at a stretch, as they were all December, lying down or half lying down, often forty-eight hours with no food but raw salt pork, sprinkled with sugar, rum and biscuit ; nothing hot, because the exhausted soldier could not collect his own fuel, as he was expected to do, to cook his own ration." Is it wonderful that, strong and intrepid as she was, Miss Nightingale was stricken down by Crimean fever and for days there was the immediate fear of death? Great was the anxiety, both at home and on the spot, but the wonderful tenacity of the patient and her good constitution carried her through, and very characteristically she absolutely refused to be sent home for convalescence. She returned for a time to Scutari and convalesced as well as she could. Truly she had her reward, for by this time the rate of mortality of the army in the Crimea had fallen from 42 per cent to 2.2 per cent of the cases treated. She had neither lived nor worked in vain. There is no wonder that the proposal to collect a Nightingale Fund was very popular and that moneys poured in, ranging from the soldiers' mites, which aggregated £9000, to large donations from wealthy individuals and communities. Miss Nightingale made it perfectly clear that any such fund should be devoted to Institutions for the training of nurses, and that it should not include anything of a personal nature.

Miss Nightingale's personal experience led her to write as follows : " What the horrors of War are no one can imagine. They are not wounds and blood and fever, spotted and low, dysentery, chronic

and acute, and cold and heat and famine. They
are intoxication, drunken brutality, demoralisation,
and disorder on the part of the inferior ; jealousies,
meanness, and indifference, selfish brutality on the
part of the superior." And all these disorders she
did not believe were inherent in the nature of the
soldier. She very rightly held that they were the
outcome of his terrible circumstances—herds of men
without wives or mothers, without proper shelter,
food or clothes, with everything to brutalise and
nothing to soften and sweeten their natures. She
was quite two generations before her time in seeing
that the soldier's faults would be best corrected by
the practical application to his hard case of Christian
charity, the provision of comforts as well as necessities and the redeeming influence of education,
amusements, and variety of life, the things for which
we all crave, and without which none of us can be
our best selves.

The War in the Crimea came to an end and the
actors, great and small, returned home, and Florence
Nightingale realised, as she had never realised before,
that her real mission, the great desire of her life,
was to make nursing a trained calling. She realised,
and so did many of her friends, among them Sidney
Herbert, the great necessity there was to act while
the British public was still eager to do something to
reward her great services and to commemorate the
sacrifice of the " heroic dead."

To secure the success of this enterprise a Royal
Commission on the Health of the Army was ap-
pointed in May 1857, and reported in February 1858.
The Chairman was her old friend, Mr, afterwards

Lord, Herbert, and the members were men who by their knowledge and enlightenment were well qualified for their work. The Report being unanimous and strongly in favour of many and much-needed reforms, the next duty was to appoint a Committee to enforce the Report. By this time the condition of her own health pointed inexorably to the *necessity* of rest and change, but it was in vain that doctors advised and friends urged this necessity on the indomitable Florence. She insisted that while she might be resting, soldiers were perishing, and that in her opinion her duty was to go on although she died for it. There is reason to believe that not only Florence Nightingale but her fellow-workers suffered to the end of her life for this heroic but tragic error of judgment, that the condition of nervous exhaustion in which she lived all the rest of her life, a period of more than fifty years, could probably have been avoided had she profited by the wisdom of the French proverb, *Reculer pour mieux sauter*. Miss Nightingale's courage, vigour, and determination carried her through the long weary years, but probably the glorious victories for the profession of nursing, for the furtherance of the soldiers' welfare, physical, moral and spiritual, her great reforms in the management of hospitals and infirmaries might have been not only more easily but more sweetly won, had her " sprite " been less at the mercy of its recalcitrant and inevitable partner. We have it from Tennyson that

> One crowded hour of glorious life
> Is worth an age without a name;

and Florence Nightingale enjoyed a working life
of well-nigh sixty years. She succeeded in almost
everything to which she set her hand. No difficulties were too great for her, and no disappointment
was considered as being more than a temporary
incident in a campaign leading to inevitable victory.
But she herself paid the penalty in dark days of
depression, remorse and weariness, and among her
many admirable fellow-soldiers in the great war
that she waged against sin and ignorance, sickness
and death, there was not one who did not at times
feel that their glorious comrade might have made the
conditions of service easier for them and for herself.

In August 1861 what she felt to be the greatest
misfortune of her life befell Florence Nightingale.
For some few months her great friend, coadjutor
and master, Lord Herbert, had been fighting against
death, and now he passed to his reward, with the
pathetic words, "Poor Florence! Poor Florence!
Our joint work unfinished!" Unfinished indeed,
but having attained such a point as to command the
crowning of their joint hopes. Even before his
death the Nightingale Training School for Nurses
was opened at St Thomas's Hospital, and a very
remarkable woman, Mrs Wardroper, was established
as its first superintendent.

She held this post for twenty-seven years and
proved herself a most able colleague and sub-
ordinate to the great Lady-in-Chief.

During the five years subsequent to her return
from the Crimea, Miss Nightingale became more
and more convinced that the condition of the civil
hospitals of England was really a larger and more

important subject than was the health of the army. From the available statistics, faulty as they were, she learned that the mortality of diseases in hospitals greatly exceeded that of the sick in their own homes. It was evident that nursing worthy of the name did not exist, and, knowing this, Miss Nightingale set herself resolutely to her work as Hospital Reformer and Founder of Modern Nursing. She had a statesman's mind and clearly saw that much improvement was needed in hospital buildings, furniture, diet, and management. Further, she was aware that this improvement was needed not only in hospitals at home, both military and civil, but also in hospitals in India and the Colonies. In addition to all this, it was clear to Miss Nightingale that true reform in hospital management could not be secured while their registers of disease and of operations were badly designed and badly kept, while there was no official list of diseases, each hospital having its own, and the Registrars, owing more to faulty systems than to derelictions of their own, omitted much that they should have entered and entered some things that did not exist. To this period belong the admirable publications on Hospitals and Nursing already mentioned. One of Miss Nightingale's enterprises did not bear immediate fruit. A School for Midwives was founded in King's College Hospital in 1861, but it had to be abandoned after some six years' working. This was, however, one of the seeds from which has resulted the enormous improvement in midwifery and in the training of midwives, which is still growing and developing at the present time.

The Reform of Workhouse Nursing came later, and her work in this direction led to association with another set of friends, one of whom, Dr Jowett, was destined to have much influence over Miss Nightingale's character and happiness in later years. The Workhouse Reform began in Liverpool, and the chief actor, under Miss Nightingale, was Mr William Rathbone, who founded a Training School and Home for Nurses in connection with the Royal Infirmary of that city. The conditions under which the sick poor were nursed under the Poor Law in those days can scarcely be realised by those of us who have only known the comfort and order which usually prevail in these institutions at the present time. The Liverpool experiment was so great a success that Miss Nightingale was encouraged to embark on a similar undertaking in London. The President of the London Poor Law Board at that time was Mr Villiers, and under him was working Mr Farnall. With this latter Florence Nightingale was soon on the best of terms. Like herself, he was a " passionate statistician," and together they collected facts, drew up and issued forms, concocted schemes, and in all ways helped Mr Villiers to secure the object they all had at heart.

No sketch of Florence Nightingale's life would be complete, nay, it would not be tolerable, without some reference to her labour of love on behalf of Indian Sanitary Reform, both military and civil. In this work she encountered difficulties that were quite special — the proud self-satisfaction of a devoted Civil Service, the ignorance and aversion to any reform common to the whole population of

K

the land, the many diversities of creed, character and race, and last, but by no means least, the unhealthiness of some of its many climates. On the other hand, as assets and encouragements the devoted woman found in successive Viceroys, Governors and enthusiastic officials the same help and support as she had obtained from many of her coadjutors in England. Florence Nightingale knew what she wanted, and fought to secure an Executive Sanitary authority in India, an Expert Control authority in London, and lastly, the publication of an Annual Report whereby public opinion in India and in England might be created and fostered. Well may Sir Edward Cook call Miss Nightingale "The Providence of the Indian Army," for we learn that in 1817 the annual death rate of the troops in India reached the appalling figure of 69 per thousand and that, by 1911, less than a hundred years later, it had fallen to the figure of 5.04 No doubt other reformers and other circumstances had contributed to this transformation, but it is only fair to remember that the reforms to which it was due were initiated by Florence Nightingale. To ensure the possession of information, and to arouse interest in this as in similar enterprises, Miss Nightingale strove for the appointment of a Royal Commission on the Sanitation of India, and one was appointed in 1859 with her great friend, Mr Herbert, as Chairman. It reported in 1863, after his death, and for some time it appeared as though this Report was still-born, although it eventually bore noble fruit, in the reduction of death rate, incidence of sickness and expenditure.

After all this record of strenuous work and hard fighting, it may be held to be something of a surprise to find the record of Florence Nightingale as a mystic. And yet why should we be astonished when we remember the strenuous lives of St Catherine of Siena, a great statesman and adviser of Popes, and the equally wonderful life of her namesake of Genoa who was herself a hospital matron? In the heading of his chapter on this subject, Sir Edward Cook quotes a short passage from Florence Nightingale herself—" Mysticism : to dwell on the unseen, to withdraw ourselves from the things of sense into communion with God—to endeavour to partake of the Divine Nature ; that is of holiness. When we ask ourselves only what is right or what is the Will of God (the same question), then we may truly be said to live in His sight."

Strangely enough, Dr Jowett was the appointed messenger to urge on her the principles that rightly govern the difficult old age which inevitably follows on a very full and strenuous life. He wrote to her : "You ought seriously to consider how your work may be carried on, not with less energy, but in a calmer spirit. Think that the work of God neither hastes nor rests and that we should go about it in the spirit of order which prevails in the world. I am not blaming the past (who would blame you who devote your life to the good of others ?) but I want the Peace of God to settle on the future." That Florence Nightingale profited by these kindly counsels, and was led to bring her will into unison with the Divine Will, is indicated by her adoption as one of her comforts in her latter days the following lines — from Sir Edwin Arnold's *The Song Celestial* :—

> Abstaining from attachment to the work,
> Abstaining from rewardment in the work,
> While yet one doeth it full faithfully,
> Saying—" 'Tis right to do," that is true act
> And abstinence ! Who doeth duties so,
> Unvexed if his work fail, if it succeed
> Unflattered, in his own heart justified,
> Quit of debates and doubts, his is " true " act.

E. Braconnie

J. M. LUDLOW

JOHN MALCOLM LUDLOW
(1821-1911)
By CHARLES E. RAVEN, D.D.

JOHN MALCOLM LUDLOW AND THE
CHRISTIAN SOCIAL MOVEMENT

" You are a Christian, certainly a Christian, and yet a democrat, a liberal, almost a socialist. That amazes me. It is not possible in my country." The professor from Louvain, my guest in 1914 at Cambridge, thus laid his finger upon what is perhaps the most precious achievement of English religion. We who are apt to grumble at the indifference of the Church to social reform, or at the failure of organised Labour to acknowledge its debt to Christianity, will do well to remember that in the countries of the Roman allegiance Catholic means reactionary and liberal is a synonym for atheist, and that in Lutheranism religion is otherworldly and individualist and has no concern with politics or the State. The Stockholm Conference of 1925 proved beyond dispute that, apart from a few enlightened and isolated thinkers, the continental nations were at least a generation behind us in their understanding of the social implications of the Gospel. Such a movement as Copec is at present impossible outside Britain. Only in the English-speaking world is a Christian democracy a conceivable ideal.

It may be that the union between Christianity and what is broadly called socialism, a union so familiar to our fellow-countrymen, is due to our national temperament, to what critics call our muddle-headedness, and friends our common sense. Certainly we have a genius for the *via media*, for avoiding clear-cut distinctions and insisting upon having our cake and eating it. And at the epoch of the revolutionary movements a hundred years ago, Methodism, sweeping over the artisan population, may well have been the main reason for our escape from violent upheavals. But while the class-war and the antagonism between religion and democracy might never have divided us as they have divided France or Russia, the construction and growth of the Christian social movement in Britain, with all that it means of ordered progress and spiritual power, are primarily due to a single and relatively obscure individual. There have been a multitude of Christian philanthropists, to whom be all honour ; a host of Christian reformers to protest against particular manifestations of evil ; it was John Malcolm Forbes Ludlow who, realising that democracy was inevitably changing the whole social tradition of mankind, first awakened the Church to the two-fold task of socialising Christianity and Christianising socialism.

When, in the third week of March 1848, he wrote from Paris, then in the throes of the February revolution, the letter to F. D. Maurice, in which he described how the socialism of Louis Blanc, beneath all its " red fool-fury," had gripped the consciences of the workers, and, unless understood by Christians, would shake their faith to its foundations, he set on foot the movement of which Maurice and Kingsley,

Westcott and Stewart Headlam, Scott Holland and
Bishop Gore are representative, the movement
which " has turned the current of our English
Christianity to the consideration of the great social
problems of the age, and is at this moment trans-
figuring the social ideals of the present." [1]

To those for whom Coleridge and Carlyle,
Maurice and Kingsley, Shaftesbury and Ruskin are
household gods, and to whom Ludlow is barely a
name, such an estimate will appear wildly ex-
aggerated. A little knowledge of the Church of the
first half of last century will reveal that, in spite of
magnificent labours for missions and the slaves, for
charity and individual consecration, there was no
attempt at all to study or influence the corporate
life of mankind, to challenge the ordering of society,
or to appreciate the ardours of reformers abroad or
Chartists at home. The old aristocratic tradition
had been undermined by the strain of the Napoleonic
wars and shattered by the Reform Act. The
general bewilderment expressed itself in the policy
Laissez-faire and the abdication even by statesmen
of the attempt to control progress. Robert Owen,
a lonely pioneer of social experiment, was a fore-
runner of Marx in his determinism and hostility to
religion. The Church, like Newman, regarded the
poor solely " as objects for compassion and benevolence." Religion came near to being what Kingsley
called it, " An opium-dose for keeping beasts of
burden patient while they were being overloaded." [2]
It was Ludlow who, as the founder of the so-called

[1] C. W. Stubbs, *Charles Kingsley*, p. 16.
[2] *Politics for the People*, p. 58.

Christian Socialist movement, by his knowledge of continental democracy, his legal training, and his long lifetime of social service, created an alliance between the champions of popular emancipation and the prophets of the Christian Gospel. Few men have done so great a work with so little overt reward.

By birth and education, character and ability, profession and length of days, he was admirably qualified for his task. Born in India on 8th March 1821, the son of a soldier, and inheriting, according to his friend, Tom Hughes, a share of the robust independence of his Cromwellian ancestor, he was left fatherless while still a child. His mother settled in Paris, and the boy was educated there, graduating B. ès. L., after a career so distinguished as to attract the attention of Guizot, then Minister of Instruction. In 1838 he came to London, read law with Bellenden Ker, and was called to the Bar in 1843. To his training he owed first and foremost his intimate acquaintance with the democratic movement. As a student he came into close touch with Fourier and the other leaders of the opposition to Louis Philippe. France was by far the most progressive country in Europe : Socialism was in the heyday of its youth : and the young Englishman was able to see beneath its rhetoric and systems the vital principles and aspirations of the people. He obtained an emancipation from convention, a passion for social righteousness, and a first-hand knowledge of schemes of reform which England could never have given. His study of constitutional history, company law and legal practice gave him

the power to adapt what he had learnt in France
to the conditions of his own country.   In addition,
he had developed a fine character, careless of praise,
free from self-seeking, unsparing of effort, persistent
in pursuit of his ends, and quick to devise appropriate
means for their attainment, and was above all a
democrat and a Christian.   In religion he had had
the advantage of working out his own position in an
atmosphere where the taboo upon the discussion of
vital issues was not so strong as in England.   He
owed much to Luther and the French Reformed
Church, to Arnold and to Coleridge.   Catholicism
in the narrow sense repelled him : the Roman
Church in the France of Louis Philippe was scarcely
calculated to attract, and Tractarianism did little
to win the favour of a friend of Maurice.   But he
was equally far from the Bible-worship of the
Evangelicals, with its concentration upon a rigid
type of personal and other-worldly piety.   For him
religion must cover the whole field of experience
and of conduct : there must be no shirking of
difficulties, no faking of arguments, no disparage-
ment of ethics, no slurring over of the claims of
Christ.   Indeed, liberal as was his outlook, the only
grounds of his disagreement with his friends arose
when he discovered in them a hesitation to cause
dissension by insisting upon the Christian basis of
their work.   He never lost the incisive logic and
fearless utterance of his French schooling ; but was
great enough to appreciate and interpret the
Christian prophet whom so many found vague,
nebulous and obscure.

His life's work may be said to have begun with

the letter from Paris in 1848, though he had previously published two volumes and taken an active part in the attack on the Corn Laws. A few days later he returned to London, met Maurice, and " the veil was parted." Thenceforward they were friends ; Ludlow had found " the only man for whom I have ever felt a sense of reverence," and Maurice had gained a follower who, by his knowledge, energy and loyalty, could lead him to apply in practice the ideals of his theology : united they formed an almost ideal combination of talents.

The fruit of their union was immediate ; and its occasion was the great Chartist fiasco of 10th April 1848. That night Ludlow, Maurice and Kingsley decided to act, and the first placard was composed. Two days later it was determined to issue a periodical and a series of tracts. *Politics for the People* appeared first on 6th May, ran through seventeen weekly numbers, Ludlow being the author of more than a third of its contents, and gave its founders not only a considerable following among the well-to-do, but a direct link with representative workers. It was followed by a series of conferences with Chartists and others, where the problems of the day were discussed and evidence of the evils of un-restricted competition accumulated. But Ludlow was not content with talk, or with a preaching which did not lead to action. His acquaintance with the efforts of the French made him eager to try similar experiments in England. During the year 1849 he was maturing his plans, revisiting Paris in the summer, investigating the *Associations*

Ouvrières organised there on Buchez's lines, and considering how their evidence bore upon British problems. Like Owen, and unlike the Rochdale pioneers, he felt that the method and conditions of production lay at the root of the evil ; that the system of private ownership, unchecked as yet by any effective combination among the workers and conducted with unrestricted and ruthless competition, could not be remedied by co-operative distribution; and that in the self-governing workshop lay the germ which, if fostered into growth, might produce a new order in industry. He set out the results of his study in the fourth Tract on Christian Socialism, and modelled upon it the scheme for Working Associations which early in 1850 he persuaded Maurice and the group to endorse. On 11th February of that year the Association of Tailors began work at 34 Castle Street, and in June the formal constitution of the movement was published.

The organisation was simple enough. At the head of it stood the Council of Promoters, with whom rested the work of propaganda, the raising of funds, the direction of policy, and " the diffusion of the principles of Co-operation as the practical application of Christianity to the purposes of trade and industry." Alongside of the Council was the Central Board or Business Committee, consisting of representatives of the workers and the managers of the several Associations, and entrusted with the settlement of details of trading, with the adjustment of relations between the Associations, and with the extension of the work. Under these were the Associations themselves, self-governing workshops, each under its own Council of Administration, acting as advisory to the manager, enrolling new Associates, and settling the internal affairs of the business. Each Associate was given an allowance, " a fair day's remuneration for a fair day's work " and proportionate to his skill; and every six months the profits, subject to deductions for repayment of loans and increase of capital, were divided among the Associates " in proportion to the time they have severally worked." Arbitrators were appointed in case of disputes between Associates and their manager, and the Central Board adjudicated as between Associations. Eight Associations constituted on these lines were at work before the close of 1850.

We have set out details of the scheme at some length because it is too often the custom to sneer at the whole programme as an amateurish venture, pious, but petty, and quite incapable of expansion. No doubt a handful of small businesses supported by a group of middle-class enthusiasts lends itself to ridicule; and if this were all, Ludlow could be dismissed in silence. But before that verdict be accepted, it must be recognised first that the undertaking was larger and more fully planned than the Co-operative Store founded at Rochdale in 1844, and that in the existing state of the law the Trade Societies were then almost equally insignificant and precarious; and secondly, that the movement thus begun very nearly succeeded in its desire to alter the whole course of industrial development. That Ludlow had framed his policy with a view to the transformation of the whole system of industry

is plain from his own repeated assertions, and
his purpose was detected by his contemporaries.
" Trade Unionism should expand into humanity,
and production be carried on by the Trade Unions,"
said Ludlow. " The Christian Socialists," wrote
W. R. Greg, his most astute opponent, " will proceed
to complete their undertaking by uniting all the
Associations in each trade into one vast guild,
governed by a central committee; and finally by
effecting a union of these guilds into one gigantic
fraternal combination : by this means the whole
industrial arrangements of society will be revolutionised." And from the first this end was patiently
followed. In 1850 a circular appealing for interest
and support had been sent to all the London
Trades Societies; and in 1851, when the Amalgamated Society of Engineers was first founded, a
definite programme was put before it and approved.
William Newton and William Allan, the two chief
figures in the A.S.E., consulted Ludlow as to the
employment in co-operative production of the
funds of the Society : a foundry, the Windsor
Ironworks in Liverpool, was selected as suitable :
a prospectus was drawn up outlining the constitution of the new venture, and the plan was
launched by the A.S.E. in September. Here was
a proposal by which Ludlow's policy, already tested
in the London workshops, might have been applied
on a large scale under the auspices of the aristocracy
of Labour. Had it succeeded the whole of the
great Trade Unions would almost certainly have
adopted it. And in a decade self-government in
industry might have been on the way to realisation.

It is testimony to the feasibility of the plan that the employers lost no time in countering it. They had watched with apprehension the formation of the huge Amalgamated Society; they were warned of the peril of a development of Association; and so in January 1852, on the trivial issue of piece-work and overtime, they declared a general lock-out. Ludlow's lectures during the ensuing strife and his articles in the *Journal of Association* show how clearly he saw the issues. Here was the first great Trade Union of the modern type engaged almost at its birth in a life-and-death struggle. What was at stake was not merely the immediate question, nor even the large matter of the power of the men to better their conditions by concerted action. The issue affected the whole future of the relations between masters and men. Was industry to develop along the lines of class-war, with every unit enrolled into the service of a vast fighting-machine? Were the Unions to devote their whole energies and funds to conflict? Or was it possible in the name of God and of His Christ not only to appeal for comradeship and a new spirit in industry, but to convince the workers that they had in Co-operative Production an instrument by which the whole system could be peacefully and effectually transformed? We hear so much in these days of the possibility of the Unions acquiring and conducting businesses for the employment of their members, and Guild Socialism has been so definitely advocated that Ludlow's movement cannot be condemned as visionary or impracticable.

It was, however, shattered by the lock-out.

Fought to a finish, it resulted not indeed in the destruction of the A.S.E. (though the men were forced to pledge themselves to give up membership), but in the loss of the funds available for the Windsor Ironworks and in the embitterment of its whole policy. Nevertheless the Christian Socialists were not prepared to accept defeat. During the lock-out two sets of engineers were established as Associations in Mile End and at the Atlas Works. Newton and the A.S.E. lent their support, and their Executive Council after the lock-out passed a resolution that " hostile resistance of Labour against Capital is not calculated to enhance the condition of the labourer, that all future operations should be directed in promoting the system of self-employment in associative workshops, as the best means of effectually regulating the conditions of labour." " We must co-operate for production," wrote Allan in a covering letter. It looked for a moment as if the new age was beginning.

It is important to set out the story of these years of Ludlow's life in some detail because it represents the standpoint from which he regarded the industrial problem and shows how nearly his policy succeeded. He was utterly convinced that the competitive system as then practised was flagrantly unchristian ; he saw that something more than improvement in conditions of hours and wages was needed ; he elaborated a programme, tested it in miniature, and strove to secure its acceptance by the organised workers. That his proposals would have prevented the mechanisation of industry with its disastrous destruction of human relationships and its de-

L

personalising of workers and employers alike, and that they were premature rather than impracticable, seems obvious enough. We who find ourselves faced with the consequences of a development which he did his best to forestall may look back wistfully upon that ancient " might have been." We cannot conceal the fact that the actual undertaking that he set on foot ended in failure.

The development of Co-operative Distribution, the impoverishment of the Promoters, the outbreak of the Crimean War, the persecution of Maurice, and the closing of several of the Associations, all contributed to the result. Subsequent experiments have demonstrated that, as compared with distribution, production is difficult to organise upon co-operative lines. It is indeed amusing to find that many of those who ardently endorse a policy close akin to Ludlow's still condemn the Christian Socialists as a band of well-intentioned idealists. Ludlow himself was wise enough to realise the root causes of the failure, and large enough to set himself to remedy them as best he could. To his mind two chief obstacles stood in his way. The former was the legal position. Association was unsheltered by law, and its members consequently at the mercy of defaulting officials. The latter, and by far the more serious, was the lack of moral qualities, of education and of mutual trust, among the workers. Schemes were feasible, if only human nature had the power to be loyal in executing them. Those two difficulties were plain.

With the law he was qualified to deal: and Slaney's Act of 1852, the great charter of Co-

operation, was his first move. Followed as it was
by further legislation, it gave him, with Hughes and
E. V. Neale, the position of trusted adviser to the
whole working-class movement. His influence,
due to his utter willingness to give the credit to
others as much as to his untiring energy and persistence, was responsible, far more largely than was
admitted, for the recognition and protection of all
the popular movements for reform.

The second task was more arduous ; and on this
he took from the first a definite line. Recognising
that vision was useless without knowledge, and
that knowledge would accomplish nothing without
moral and spiritual power, he threw himself
from the first into educational and religious
work. He had written voluminously in the
various publications of the Christian Socialists and,
where permitted, in the general press. And in 1854,
when, as Kingsley put it, his experience of the
Associations had proved that " it will take two
generations of training " before the workers are
ready for co-operation, he joined with Maurice,
Hughes, Furnivall and others to set up the Working
Men's College, which still flourishes in Crowndale
Road, Camden Town,[1] and with which he was
actively connected for many years until a grave
alteration of policy, carried against him by Furnivall,
forced him to give up his work. In this case as in
others, where he criticised members of the group,
the difficulty arose over the place of religion in the
movement. Like Maurice, Ludlow believed and
stated freely that only in Christ, as men realised

[1] It was originally opened in Red Lion Square.

their unity in Him and bowed to His obedience, could there be the power for a righteous social life. In morality without religion he had little confidence, and his conviction that the basal problems of corporate life were rather moral than economic was confirmed by his experience of the Associations. Under such circumstances he resisted any attempt to conceal or diminish the prime importance of Christianity. To do so might secure the accession of men of goodwill to the movement : it might win publicity and popularity for the work : but it was none the less a disaster and almost a betrayal of the central responsibility, and would in fact defeat the very ends for which it was advocated. Just as he always insisted that the mainspring of Christian Socialism was the weekly Bible reading with Maurice, so he stood firm for the proclamation that the work was unashamedly Christian, and depended from first to last upon Christian faith and Christian practice. Neale and others of the group were anxious not to let matters of doctrine or even of belief prevent the supporters of co-operation from joining them on equal terms. They took the view that to create barriers and to exclude zealous workers by brandishing before them the claims of religion was unwise and possibly uncharitable. Ludlow on that issue could not yield ; and in this respect often stood alone. Unlike Maurice he had no fear of efficiency or of system : indeed, from the first he advocated a business-like organisation. But where Maurice was content to let his own character speak for him, Ludlow would assent to nothing which tended to place religion in a secondary position or to allow the religious motive to be taken for granted. He preferred a small band of convinced believers, a power-house of spiritual life, to a larger and less united movement. Probably his French training, and the atmosphere in which he had hammered out his philosophy of life, set him free from the shyness and reticence of his colleagues : but probably also he saw more clearly than they that the vast reform of which he dreamed would make too large demands on human altruism to be carried out except by men wholly consecrated. He believed that with Christ the transformation was possible, but that it could not be achieved on any other lines. He was overruled. Holyoake and Furnivall took his place as leaders in co-operation and workers' education. Looking back over the history of half a century it is difficult not to feel that after all Ludlow was right. We have schemes in abundance, and an abundance of vague goodwill. We still very evidently lack the power which religion alone can supply.

We have concentrated attention upon this relatively brief episode in his life, because it represents not only the crucial period in his own story, but a critical event in the history of Christianity in England. To Ludlow's work in the six years from 1848 to 1854 may be traced the origin of the whole social activities of the Church. From the theology of Hort to the housing schemes of Octavia Hill, from the " muscular Christianity " of Kingsley to the impassioned sociology of Ruskin, Ludlow's influence is manifest. His Associations may have failed : his hopes have been disappointed : he himself died almost unsung. But he had bridged the gulf between Christianity and Labour and left disciples more numerous than that of any Churchman of his time.

Yet to stop at 1854 is to deal with little more than a third of his life, and to suggest that his influence stopped with the disbanding of the Christian Socialists. For the next fifteen years he devoted himself to professional, literary and philanthropic work, marrying in 1869 Miss Maria Forbes, and living at Wimbledon in a house adjoining that of Tom Hughes. In 1870 he was made secretary of the Royal Commission on the Friendly Societies, and after the publication of the Report was appointed Registrar, an office which he held from 1875 to 1891. In this capacity he was brought into the closest personal contact with the best brains and hearts among the workers as well as with the officials of the Home Office, and in both directions was able to exert an authority which, if anonymous and unrecognised by the public, was a very real force in the development of social life. After his retirement he continued public work and contributed largely to the *Economic Review*, the organ of the Christian Social Union, and to the advocacy of co-partnership. In 1908 he made a last speech in public at the Church Congress to protest against any narrowing of the large word Socialism and to claim that the Christian Socialism which Maurice preached was the faith of all his audience. He died on 11th October 1911, being then ninety years old but still in full possession of his faculties and still eager to know and follow God's will for him.

The greatness of the man comes out in the bare record of those long years of patient and systematic labour. To be content, after inspiring a great movement, to settle down to unromantic and un- recognised service in what was for a man of such power a humble sphere ; to devote himself, after he had tried to effect reform by frontal attack, to the steady development of moral and physical welfare among the workers ; to yield to others, or rather to insist upon bestowing upon them, the credit for what he had inspired and achieved ; to keep clear and fresh the ideals of his youth, and to merit " the veneration of all who had served with him in any capacity " ; [1] and to live to see the fruit of his efforts manifesting itself in a change of public and religious opinion which he could describe in 1892 as " some- thing perfectly marvellous "—this testifies to a char- acter as fine as it is rare.

He was the first Churchman of the industrial age to see clearly that Christianity has a double task to perform. Before him attention had been con- centrated solely upon the individual, alike by those who accepted and by those who deplored the break- down of the old social order. He realised that, alongside of conversion and spiritual liberty, the Church must stand for political emancipation and industrial liberty, for the true democracy which he defines as " the giant self-control of a nation, ruling itself as one man, in wisdom and righteousness, beneath the eye of God." [2] To that end he formulated the scheme of Co-operative Production,

---

[1] So his successor, Sir Edward Brabrook.
[2] *Christian Socialist*, i. p. 49.

believing that it would conserve the human relationships in industry, train the workers in fellowship and self-government, and transform the whole basis of society from one of class antagonism to one of mutual service. Realising that the time for such change was not yet, he was ready to wait until he could devote himself to the sort of career in which he could best foster the moral responsibility and general well-being of the workers. Having found it he spent his powers in guiding and befriending the societies which more perhaps than any others are educationally valuable. He had decided that neither politics nor public movements were likely to succeed unless the defects which his experience had detected in the human material were remedied. Above all, he dreaded the advent of the servile State where men should become comfortable pensioners of a plutocracy and sell their souls for a mess of pottage. And to the last he gave himself to building up a population which should realise that, in the words of the first placard of 1848, " there will be no true freedom without virtue, no true science without religion, no true industry without the fear of God and love to your fellow-citizens."

WILLIAM MORRIS

WILLIAM MORRIS (1834-96)

By HUGH MARTIN, M.A.

WILLIAM MORRIS

THE life of William Morris (1834–1896) roughly covered the Victorian era. He was one of the greatest of the great men of that age for which the Georgians are so fond of exercising vicarious humility, and—like many of the great Victorians —he was all his life in revolt against all that we call Victorianism. His father was a wealthy bill-broker, and Morris's childhood was spent in a large house on the edge of Epping Forest, where he acquired a passion for Nature that never left him. At the age of thirteen he went to Marlborough, where he neither played nor worked, but took his own line. His schoolfellows knew him as a strange youth who mooned about by himself, read pro-digiously, and told long stories " full of knights and fairies."

When he went to Oxford at the age of nineteen he continued to educate himself. He acquired little from his tutors except a profound contempt for the whole educational system. To the end of his days the word " don " remained a term of the strongest abuse and a synonym for all that was narrow, ignorant and pedantic. His tutor, on the other hand, described Morris as a rather rough, unpolished youth who exhibited no special literary tastes or capacity. Oxford itself captured his heart by its beauty, but it was as a treasure from the past that he loved it, not as a power in the present. In the first two or three days there he made friends with Edward Burne-Jones, a freshman from Birmingham who already showed promise as an artist, but who—like Morris—was preparing for ordination in the Anglican Church. It was a friendship that lasted till death and profoundly influenced the lives of both.

From the first Morris regarded life as a trust, and, though possessed of a private income of £900 a year, saw in his freedom from the necessity of earning a living only an opportunity for unfettered choice of his life-work. Before he took his degree he decided, in company with Burne-Jones, to become an artist and not a priest. At Oxford he had made the discovery that he was able to write poetry. A college friend of his tells of a visit paid one evening to Morris and Burne-Jones. As soon as he entered the room Burne-Jones exclaimed wildly, "He's a great poet." "Who is?" "Why, Topsy!" (Morris was called "Topsy" after the child in *Uncle Tom's Cabin*, because of his mop of curly hair.) Then Morris read them the first poem he had ever written. To their outspoken admiration he replied, "Well, if this is poetry it is very easy to write!" And for a term or two he produced a new poem nearly every day.

It is tempting to dwell upon Morris as a poet, and linger in the romantic world of his stories and lyrics, but our present purpose calls us to follow other aspects of his life, and we must dismiss his greatest gift in a few words. He was a fertile and a musical writer, and as a story-teller he is perhaps supreme among our modern poets. " In all the noble roll of our poets," said Swinburne, " there has been since Chaucer no second teller of tales comparable to the first till the advent of this one." Had Morris produced nothing more than his poetry we should still have marvelled at his output and energy. His writings fill many volumes and entitle him to rank with the greatest. But great as is the poet's calling, and great as was Morris's achievement in it, he was not the type of man to be content with a life of studious leisure and merely literary activity.

Morris's decision, in his last year at Oxford, to become an architect was one which revealed the main purpose of his life, although his actual connection with the profession was very brief. All his subsequent many-sided activity might be described as an attempt to create homes fit for human beings to inhabit. All the crafts to which he turned his hand—painting, furniture-making, weaving, dyeing—were consciously subservient to this end. The only possible exception was his later love of printing.

Here then we note the first great principle of Morris's life : his love and concern for the Home. Though he never practised as an architect, and never built a house, yet it might almost be said that all his life he was doing nothing else. Speaking of a lecture he was preparing on the prospects of architecture in modern civilisation, he once wrote that the subject " seems to me the most serious that a man can think of ; for 'tis no less than the chances of a calm, dignified and therefore happy life for the mass of mankind." The house is the material framework of the home, and nothing can recompense a man, still more a woman, for a sordid, overcrowded, unhealthy home. The physical, moral and spiritual degradation caused by bad housing is writ large upon the whole fabric of modern civilisation. " To him," says his biographer, " the man lived in the house almost as the soul lives in the body. The degradation of architecture and of its subservient arts of decoration was at once the cause and the effect of the whole degradation of human life." [1] He was never weary of insisting upon the importance of living in beautiful surroundings, and equally insistent that such beauty should be and could be made possible for everyone. " Have nothing in your houses that you do not know to be useful or believe to be beautiful," was his fundamental maxim. There are few houses still, and there were even fewer in Morris's day, where the application of that rule would not work wonders. The accumulation of useless and usually ugly furniture and ornament is a vice of all classes, and dulls the very sense of beauty. By beauty Morris meant something very different from luxury : only one feature of civilisation moved him to more sorrow and wrath than did the housing of the poor, and that was the housing of the rich. Vulgarity in furniture was to him a symptom of a wrong state of mind. " A society which worships riches will express its

[1] J. W. Mackail, *William Morris*, ii. 67.

idolatry even in its table legs and chandeliers." [1]
He was once contemptuously described as a poetic
upholsterer. Morris welcomed the phrase. He
thought that upholstery and furniture could be
poetical and that they ought to be. In his vision
of the future he foreshadowed and helped to create
the modern Town Planning and Garden Cities
Movement. "I want neither the towns to be
appendages of the country nor the country of the
town : I want the town to be impregnated with
the beauty of the country and the country with
the intellectual and vivid life of the town. I want
every homestead to be clean and orderly and tidy—
a lovely house surrounded by acres and acres of
garden. On the other hand, I want the town to
be clean, orderly and tidy—in short, a garden with
beautiful houses in it. Clearly if I don't wish this
I must be a fool or a dullard ; but I do more—I
claim it as the due heritage of the latter ages of
the world which have subdued nature, and can
have it for the asking." [2]

Morris began with his own home. When he
married he determined to create a house which
should exemplify his ideals. When it was built
he set about furnishing it, only to find that he
could get nothing in the shops which he would
allow inside its doors. So he began to design, and
to get his friends to design, his furniture. But he
found it almost impossible even to get the articles
made as he wanted them. Accordingly he determined to make them himself, and, with several

[1] Clutton Brock, *William Morris*, p. 63.
[2] Mackail, ii. 321.

friends, including Rossetti, Maddox Brown and Burne-Jones, he founded the firm of Morris, Marshall, Faulkner & Co., whose influence has affected all the domestic arts of the Western world.

The story of the progress of the business through its early struggles to commercial success is fascinating, and in them all Morris was the moving spirit. The first circular of the firm insisted upon the necessity of the co-operation of the artist and the workman, that indeed the two must become one. " From the first," wrote Rossetti, " the firm turned out whatever anyone wanted in the way of decorative material—architectural adjuncts, furniture, tapestries, embroideries, stained glass, wall papers and what not. The goods were first-rate, the art and the workmanship excellent, the prices high. . . . You could have the things such as the firm chose that they should be, or you could do without them. . . . There was no compromise. Morris, as senior partner, laid down the law and all his clients had to bend or break." Morris had a ferocious temper, and he sometimes visited it on customers who wished to insist upon what he considered inartistic and unworthy. He listened with growing impatience on one occasion to a wealthy lady client who was criticising some of his colour schemes, and at last burst out, as he turned away in disgust, " If you want dirt, you can find plenty of it in the street outside."

Morris was not only the manager, giving orders; he was the working foreman. He said in a letter to a friend that he had become " a master artisan, if I may claim that dignity." To each industry in turn he gave his undivided attention, studying not only design but materials and execution. He spent days designing wall papers and chintzes and devising the best methods of printing them. " I am trying to learn all I can about dyeing, even the handiwork of it, which is simple enough ; but like many other simple things contains matters in it that one would not think of unless one were told. Besides my business of seeing to the cotton printing I am working in the dye-house in sabots and blouse pretty much all day long." He not only became an expert dyer : he worked for days at the loom and re-invented the lost art of tapestry weaving. And all the while he kept writing poetry, with time to spare for fun and holidays and friendship. He had found work to do that was worth doing, and he rejoiced with all his soul in the doing of it. Though financial success came, he carried on the business not because he wished to make money, but because he wished to make the things he manufactured.

Here we arrive at the second of the great principles on which Morris's whole philosophy was founded—the first being his love for the home— namely, that the root of all our troubles and the hope of our future lay in men's attitude to work. He insisted that the doing of a piece of work well for its own sake, and finding pleasure in the doing of it, was at once the secret of true living and of true art. The essential aim of commerce should be the making of goods, and not the making of profit for the manufacturer on the one hand or

M

the finding of employment for the working classes
on the other. Morris recognised no essential distinction between the artist and the workman.
Until artists were workmen and workmen artists
no living art could exist. He was full of scorn for
" the quasi-artistic members of the middle classes,"
who propounded schemes for producing art without realising that the roots of art were gone. Art
for him did not mean merely painting and sculp-
ture, but any work which a workman does with
love for his job. Art is man's expression of his
joy in labour, and Morris believed this joy in
labour to be the thing best worth having in life.
" It is right and necessary," he insisted, " that all
men should have work of itself pleasant to do ;
nay more, work done without pleasure is, however
one may turn it, not real work at all, but useless
and degrading toil. . . . No work which cannot
be done with pleasure in the doing is worth doing."
Speaking once of the depravity visible in the faces,
manners and speech of the holiday crowds that
went past his home at Hammersmith, he blamed
their brutality upon the life they had to lead. " I
know by my own feelings and desires what these
men want, what would have saved them from this
lowest depth of savagery : employment which
would foster their self-respect and win praise and
sympathy of their fellows, and dwellings which
they could come to with pleasure, surroundings
which would soothe and elevate them ; reasonable labour, reasonable rest." In a civilised community the reward of the worker should be just
what Morris claimed for himself : " Money

enough to keep him from fear of want and degradation for him and his; leisure enough from bread-earning work (even though it be pleasant to him) to give him time to read and think and connect his own life with the life of the great world; work enough of the kind aforesaid and praise of it, and encouragement enough to make him feel good friends with his fellows; and lastly (not least, for 'tis verily part of the bargain) his own due share of art, the chief part of which will be a dwelling that does not lack the beauty which Nature would freely allow it, if our own perversity did not turn Nature out of doors." " It cannot be too often repeated that the true incentive to useful and happy labour is and must be pleasure in the work itself." "That simple sentence," writes Mr Mackail, " contains the sum of his belief in politics, in economics, in art." [1]

But when Morris looked at society and the workaday life of men, he found it as far from expressing his ideal as men's houses were. " It may well be a burden to the conscience of an honest man who lives a more manlike life to think of the innumerable lives which are spent in toil unrelieved by hope and uncheered by praise; men who might as well, for all the good they are doing their neighbours by their work, be turning a crank with nothing at the end of it. . . . Over and over again have I asked myself why should not my lot be the common lot ? My work is simple work enough; much of it, nor that the least pleasant, any man of decent intelligence could do

[1] ii. 257.

if he could but get to care about the work and
its results. Indeed, I have been ashamed when I
have thought of the contrast between my happy
working hours and the unpraised, unrewarded,
monotonous drudgery which most men are condemned to. Nothing shall convince me that
such labour as this is good or necessary to
civilisation."

It was not poverty that made Morris rebel so
much as the work that men had to do. He wanted
far more than a redistribution of wealth. If
extreme poverty and extreme riches had been
abolished, and men still worked at the same tasks
and in the same fashion as they did before, Morris
would have felt that little progress had been made.
" Men did what was not worth doing so that they
might live, and lived so that they might do what
was not worth doing." [1] Such futility grated on
his soul. How could men live manly lives under
such conditions ? " If I were to work ten hours
a day at work I despised and hated I should spend
my leisure, I hope, in political agitation, but I
fear in drinking."

He could not feel that all this was a matter of
indifference to him merely because his own lot in
life was pleasant. The burden on his conscience
became heavier. "Do you know, when I see a
poor devil drunk and brutal I always feel, quite
apart from my æsthetical perceptions, a sort of
shame, as if I myself had some hand in it." And
from all the beauty there was in the world the mass
of men were shut out.

[1] A. Clutton Brock.

"The singers have sung and the builders have builded,
The painters have fashioned their tales of delight;
For what and for whom hath the world's book been
    gilded
When all is for these but the blackness of night?"

So there fell upon his ear "with ever-increasing
urgency the cry of a bewildered and unhappy
people,"[1] and in the hope that he might do something to redeem them he gave up ease and leisure
and much of what made life most desirable to him.
He became a rebel against society not because of
his own unhappiness, but because others could not
share the happiness that was his. His own comfort
and joy became intolerable to him.

Mr Clutton Brock has drawn an interesting
parallel between the careers of Ruskin and Morris.
The badness of the building and applied art of
his time distressed Ruskin because art was not to
him a superfluity which men could have or not as
they chose, a pleasant frill upon the substance of
life. It was a quality of everything that men
made, and it was good or bad according to the
goodness or badness of the workers. So from
being a critic of art, Ruskin became a critic of
society; "after writing about old buildings and
modern painters, he wrote about political economy,
about the order and disorder of the society which
produced all the ugliness of his own time. . . . As
Ruskin turned from the criticism of works of art
to the criticism of society, so William Morris
turned from the making of works of art to the

[1] Mackail, ii. 32.

effort to remake society." [1] Because he was an artist, Morris was driven to become a social reformer.

So in the autumn of 1882 Morris, now forty-eight years of age, joined the Democratic Federation (afterwards the Social Democratic Federation and later the British Socialist Party). As in his craftsmanship so in his politics he threw himself whole-heartedly into the business of propaganda. He tried to study Marx. He wrote numerous socialist tracts, articles and poems. He edited and financed socialist papers, spent hours in committee, addressed all kinds of audiences—in halls and back-rooms and at street corners. Much of this—and especially the speaking, which he never liked and for which he had no gift—went sadly against the grain. Even more distasteful were the internal dissensions and jealousies of socialist politics into which he was drawn. But he felt, like Paul, that he had a message which must be voiced: "Woe is me if I preach not the Gospel." He sacrificed health and leisure and interests and put his hand deeply into his pocket. He sold most of his valuable and well-loved books for the funds of the Federation. To tell the story would take long and serve little purpose, but it is worth while to try to understand his thoughts and feelings.

His decisive action, of course, reflected itself at once in all his utterances. He lectured on "Art, Wealth and Riches" in Manchester soon after joining the Federation, and used the occasion to preach socialism, to the anger of his audience.

[1] Clutton Brock, 14 f.

They were prepared to hear him on art, but this was another matter altogether. " No," replied Morris, " I specially wished to point out that the question of popular art was a social question, involving the happiness or misery of the greater part of the community. The absence of popular art from modern times is more disquieting and grievous to bear for this reason than for any other, that it betokens that fatal division of men into the cultivated and the degraded classes which competitive commerce has bred and fosters ; popular art has no chance of a healthy life, or indeed of a life at all, till we are on the way to fill up this terrible gulf between riches and poverty. . . . What business have we with art at all unless all can share it ? "

He was impatient with Radicals, who were concerned, he thought, merely with political change, while accepting the existing order of society. It seemed to him that the whole basis of society and its contrasts of rich and poor were incurably vicious. " All political change seems to me useful now as making it possible to get the social one." " I can see no use in people having political freedom unless they use it as an instrument for leading reasonable and manlike lives ; there is no good even in education, if when they are educated people have only slavish work to do, and have to live lives too much beset with sordid anxiety for them to be able to think and feel with the more fortunate people who produce art and poetry and great thoughts. This release from slavery, it is clear, cannot come to people so long as they are subjected to the bare subsistence wages which are a necessity of competitive commerce." For state socialism as a political system he had little use either, believing that it was not nearly fundamental enough. Drastic change was necessary and drastic action to secure it. He often declared that he had no interest in any kind of politics but revolutionary politics. " The contrasts of rich and poor," he wrote to a friend, " are unendurable and ought not to be endured by either rich or poor. Now it seems to me that feeling this I am bound to act for the destruction of the system which seems to me mere oppression and destruction. Such a system can only be destroyed by the united discontent of numbers, isolated acts of a few persons of the middle and upper classes seeming to me quite powerless against it : in other words, the antagonism of classes which the system has bred is the natural and necessary instrument for its destruction." His theories as to social structure are perhaps hardly worth detailed examination. Apparently he wanted " a federation of communities holding wealth in common " ; *News from Nowhere* is an imaginative picture of his ideal. He was not a political thinker but a prophet.

His faith was that if only men had the right ideals they would soon discover ways and means to achieve them. " Our business is the making of socialists, *i.e.* convincing people that socialism is good for them and is possible. When we have enough people of that way of thinking they will find out what action is necessary for putting their principles in practice. Therefore, I say, make socialists. We socialists can do nothing else that is useful." Education was what was needed, the inculcation of new ideals. Only a change of heart could bring about this ideal society. Men must have new values and new standards of life. "Fellowship is life," he preached through the lips of John Ball, "and lack of fellowship is death." He believed that men could redeem society if they wanted to : that the present order with its injustice and oppression was evil and unnecessary and could be done away. He wanted to arouse and focus the discontent of the masses, and he saw, as prophets are apt to do, the revolution he desired near at hand. The task of socialists was so to work as to make the change come with as little confusion and suffering as might be. "Education towards revolution seems to me to express in three words what our policy should be." He stood aloof from parliamentarians on the one hand and from anarchists who believed in immediate bombs and barricades on the other.

He found few to stand by him in his policy. Eventually he had to resign from the Federation, which soon after collapsed. Undeterred, Morris founded another, The Hammersmith Socialists' Society, which never had a large membership. His enthusiasm for the cause never relaxed, but he came to feel that the active work of propaganda was unsuited to his powers, and his health also began to fail. For the last seven years of his life he withdrew from its stress and turmoil, though he still lectured and wrote for his social ideals.

His last great activity was found in the new craft to which he now turned his hand, that of printing. Though books play so great a part in modern life, there are unhappily few who think of printing as more than a means of multiplying copies, or see beauty in a well-printed page or a seemly binding. Yet a beautiful, readable type, printed with proper margins on good paper, provides the only fitting setting for worthy prose or verse. The beauty of good printing does not lie in added ornaments or designs, but in the printing itself, in the performing well of the function of printing, the clear, readable reproduction of the author's message. By the type faces he designed, and the books turned out by his Kelmscott Press, Morris did much to contribute to the higher standard of printing which is happily common to-day.

How shall one attempt to sum up such a man! If the sketch of his doings and thoughts here attempted has failed to conjure up his portrait, no concluding paragraph can hope to succeed. He was a remarkable combination of the seer, " the dreamer of dreams "—as he described himself— and the man of action overflowing with practical energy. Whatever may be thought of his political schemes, his dreams still live, and by capturing the hearts of men they have contributed and will still contribute to weaving the substance of the world to be. But his practical activities, too, have played a great part in remoulding the life of the world, and many of us in these days enjoy the benefits of his labour without knowing whence they come. The amount of work he did in litera-

ture, in art, in politics was enough to fill the lives
of several ordinary men. His super-abundant
creative energy was ever on the search for new
tasks. No sooner had he mastered one craft than
he passed on to another. His whole-heartedness
in the task of the moment was manifest, but all his
tasks were part of the main purpose of his life—
the building of a commonwealth of free, healthy,
happy comrades. He had his faults of vision and
temper, as who has not, but his life's aim was
fundamentally unselfish, and to it he gave himself
and all he had unsparingly. " I have no hesitation in saying," wrote his family doctor, " that
he died a victim to his enthusiasm for spreading
the principles of socialism." " The disease," said
another doctor who attended him at the end, " is
simply being William Morris and having done
more work than most ten men."

He died on October 3, 1896, at the age of
sixty-three. His body was buried in the little
churchyard at Kelmscott, carried there in a farm
wagon driven by a countryman.

There is little in his writings about religious
belief. He was more reticent than most men
about such questions. But who can doubt that
he was one who set first the Kingdom of God and
His righteousness. I can picture to myself his
surprise at his welcome in the celestial city.
" Lord," he would say, " when saw I thee in prison
and came unto thee ? " And the King would
make answer, " Inasmuch as ye sought to free these
my brethren, ye did it unto me."

GEORGE CADBURY

GEORGE CADBURY (1839-1922)

By H. G. WOOD, M.A.

GEORGE CADBURY [1]

Give us to build, above the deep intent,
The deed, the deed.

THE failure to convert intent into deed which is apparent in the life of many a social reformer may be due not to weakness of will, as this is ordinarily understood, but to the impatience of the idealist who shuns the drudgery of detail and who lacks the instinctive perception of the right thing to do at any given moment. Judgment and attention to detail lie at the root of practical achievement. These qualities were essential factors in George Cadbury's contribution to social progress. That contribution consisted not in the theoretic elabora-

---

[1] Anyone who writes about George Cadbury must rely on Mr A. G. Gardiner's admirable biography, which first appeared in 1923 and which may now also be obtained in a smaller illustrated edition (1925). My references are to this edition.

Mrs George Cadbury very kindly placed at my disposal some of the papers which had already been in Mr Gardiner's hands. From these I have taken one or two fresh illustrations of George Cadbury's outlook, but he who gleans after Mr Gardiner must expect a thin harvest.

It was my privilege to enjoy George Cadbury's friendship and to be associated with him particularly in the work of religious education. Of this side of his interests I have said but little in the text, as it hardly came within the limits set to the article. But through my personal contacts with him I learned to appreciate the wisdom of his judgments and his amazing thoughtfulness for others.

tion of ideas, but in their concrete embodiment in deeds. He created a new type of factory and he built a new type of garden-village. It was thus by practical example that he showed how wages might be raised in a modern industry and how something like Jerusalem might be builded not *among* dark Satanic mills, but *in* mills that were no longer dark or Satanic. In the same way, he demonstrated in Bournville how our housing conditions might be revolutionised. This he could not have done, if he had not been alive to the importance of detail, and if he had not possessed a certain indefinable capacity of judgment. These characteristics are the foundation of business enterprise. To many, the significance and value of the reforms with which George Cadbury was identified are obscured by the fact that he was a successful business man and made money. But the same qualities which led to his success as a manufacturer underlie his success as a social reformer. If he had not been a great entrepreneur, he could not have been a great philanthropist, or a great pioneer in big causes.

George Cadbury was a Quaker, and came of Quaker stock. He was born on 19th September 1839, in a house in Calthorpe Road, Edgbaston, Birmingham, and he owed much to the Quaker-Evangelical tradition of the home in which he was brought up. Quakerism was cradled in a distrust of notions and theories, and in a concern for the practical interpretation of Christianity. The Quaker atmosphere would reinforce the practical bent of George Cadbury's mind. As a true Quaker, he would ask, in relation to every problem, what can be done, and, still more, what can be done immediately ? He would, moreover, be predisposed by his Quaker inheritance to a step-by-step philosophy. It is part of the Quaker faith that when a problem as a whole seems insoluble, there is some step open to us at once, and if that step be taken, the next will be made clear to us. We may not ask to see the distant scene and we must learn to say, "one step enough for me." Thoroughness and attention to detail were also inculcated in the Quaker-Puritan morality. Along with this went simplicity of life, a subordination of recreation to duty and of play to work, which led to seriousness of purpose and concentration of interest. A. G. Gardiner points out more than once how the whole energy of George Cadbury's nature was directed into a few well-marked channels, and how essential this concentration of interest was to the work he accomplished. Associated with the step-by-step philosophy to which I have just referred, was the power of accepting responsibility without anxiety. Some eighteenth-century Friends made use of the term "Freecare" as a personal name. It expressed a quality which they admired. The spirit of quiet confidence which comes through being able to cast one's care on God has had a great deal to do with anything Quakers have accomplished. This spirit George Cadbury possessed in no small measure.[1]

[1] A remarkable illustration of this same capacity to bear responsibility without anxiety may be found in the life of Lord Salisbury :—

"Another revealing speech can be recalled. It was when he was Foreign Minister and at a moment of acute international

N

In the first half of the nineteenth century Quakerism was responding to the quickening touch of the Evangelical Revival, and in the person of a leader like Joseph Sturge was becoming alive to the appeal of great humanitarian and democratic causes. Evangelical enthusiasm and humanitarian sympathy alike found their outlet in the Adult School movement which Joseph Sturge introduced into Birmingham in 1845. Into the work of an Adult School George Cadbury entered whole-heartedly as a young man; he continued in the movement as an active teacher for over forty years, and he never lost his interest in it. What the

crisis. He had been entertaining guests at Hatfield and expressed relief at their departure as freeing him from a certain embarrassment. They had all been very kind, he said, in condoling with him upon the burden of responsibility under which he must be labouring, and he had not known how to answer them : ' They would have been so terribly shocked if I had told them the truth —which was that I didn't understand what they were talking about.' There were exclamations of protest from members of his family and he proceeded to explain further. He was about to start upon a walk and was standing at the moment at the open door, looking out upon the threatening clouds of an autumn afternoon. ' I don't understand,' he repeated, ' what people mean when they talk of the burden of responsibility. I should understand if they spoke of the burden of decision—I feel it now, trying to make up my mind whether or no to take a great-coat with me. I feel it in exactly the same way, but no more, when I am writing a despatch upon which peace or war may depend. Its degree depends upon the materials for decision that are available and not in the least upon the magnitude of the results which may follow.' Then, after a moment's pause and in a lower tone, he added, ' With the results I have nothing to do.' "— *Life*, Vol. I., p. 118. George Cadbury similarly often felt the burden of decision, but the decision once made, he could face the consequences with equanimity.

Adult School meant to him is clearly indicated in the following letter :—

" It was most helpful to me because I saw that religion was something really practical that brought joy and peace with it. Some people disbelieve that Jesus Christ cast out devils. I have seen this so often done by His Spirit that there is no difficulty to me to believe. Scores of men have come into our Class bad-tempered and selfish. I have in my mind two or three stiffly-built fellows who were dreaded by the police because they were very strong and the police had to suffer when they dealt with them. The drinking, bad-tempered devils were cast out, and these men became gentle, loving fathers and husbands. I have seen selfish men with the selfish devil cast out become unselfish ; drunken men with the drink devil cast out, become sober and thoughtful ; gambling men with the gambling devil cast out, spend the money, once wasted on gambling, on their wives and children. I have seen thieves and house-breakers give up their business—they told me that I had no conception of the difficulty it was to them, because it was such exciting sport to break into a house with the uncertainty as to what might be found, and because of the pleasure that the danger and risk gave them, and yet they abandoned their thieving and became good citizens ; one house-breaker that I sent over to Canada asked me : ' How can I possibly get back my good name ? ' I advised him to go to Canada and live it down ; he wrote me a few years after to say that he had followed my advice and now was doing well there.

" Then, it is delightful to think of miserable, wretched homes turned into happy Christian homes, and the man who was unhappy before, tho' self-indulgent, ' filled with all peace and joy in believing.' "

The influence which George Cadbury himself exerted as a teacher is perhaps sufficiently illus-

trated by a letter received from an old scholar in
1901 :—

"It is just forty-four years to-day since I joined your
Class. While in your Class, it was a very critical part of
my history. I had a father sadly given to drink, which
brought its usual discouragements, making it exceeding
hard to live against it. But your interest in me and kindly
visits to my home did not lose its helpfulness ; but most
of all your kneeling on our quarried floor in Bell Barn Road
in earnest prayer left its indelible stamp on my memory.
That 'still water ran deep' ; forty-four years' struggle has
not erased its blessed influence."

This letter brings out two elements in George
Cadbury's power as a teacher, his practice of
visiting the members of his school in their homes
and his readiness to pray with them and for them.
We may also note his belief in what he called a
simple gospel. His teaching was undogmatic in
the sense that he laid no stress on creeds. He
thought the appeal of Christ could always be put
into some simple practical form. "I do not ask
what a man believes. If he is a drunkard, let him
put away the drink ; if he is a gambler, let him
put away the gambling ; if he is a domestic tyrant,
let him govern his temper." [1] It is hardly necessary to point out that, in this emphasis on the
practical test of Christianity, George Cadbury was
in line with the true Quaker tradition. So far as
he could, George Cadbury made his school a source
of practical help to all who came to it, and a place
in which each one found something to do and
could express himself in service.

[1] *Life*, p. 48.

The intimate contact with the homes of his scholars aroused and sustained George Cadbury's interest in housing. In an interview reported in the *Christian Commonwealth* in 1898, he put the matter thus : "Forty years ago I visited among my scholars and knew their hardships and the difficulties men have to contend with when they are reformed—unattractive neighbourhoods, no social life and but few objects of interest in and around their homes. But if each man could have his own house, a large garden to cultivate and healthy surroundings—then, I thought, there will be for them a better opportunity of a happy family life." Later, in reply to a questionnaire issued by Bishop Gore, he again brought out the connection between his adult school work and his convictions about housing. "Largely through my experience among the back streets of Birmingham I have been brought to the conclusion that it is impossible to raise a nation, morally, physically, and spiritually in such surroundings, and that the only effective way is to bring men out of the cities into the country and to give to every man his garden where he can come into touch with nature and thus know more of nature's God."[1] It may be worth while to note in passing that George Cadbury was not troubled by the antithesis of personal evangelism and social reform which has bothered so many Christians, particularly of the Evangelical school. To change men's hearts and to change their homes were parts of the same task, and the Christian has not to ask which comes first or which is the more

[1] *Life*, p. 107.

important, but to take his share in either line of work as he may be guided.

To George Cadbury's mind, the housing-problem and the problem of the ownership and control of land which is inextricably bound up with housing were the most important issues in social reform. In addressing some members of the Trades Union Congress in Hanley in 1905, he said: " The evils [of poverty] will never be cured by the prohibition of liquor or of betting—the twin curses of Great Britain to-day. Even if these evils were prohibited, other evils would arise while men live in the depressing and demoralising surroundings they do. True Radicals must go to the root of the matter, as our name implies—that is, I believe, land monopoly." This was a considered judgment. He thought a good garden the best counter-attraction to the public-house, and the interests which gather round a garden the most effective antidote to gambling. Houses with adequate gardens would prove, he was convinced, the most economical way of using land. The intensive cultivation of the garden meant that land used for providing adequate homes would actually produce more foodstuffs than the same land if used for pasture or agriculture. The land would thus increasingly become the storehouse of the poor instead of being the playground of the rich.

While he thus regarded housing reform as fundamental, he did not dissociate it from changes in industry. No improvements in housing would be possible unless tenants could pay for better houses. This pointed to the necessity of raising wages. George Cadbury believed in the principle of a legally enforced minimum wage. But he was first resolved to see what could be done to raise wages by improved factory organisation. It was in this way that what he did in transforming the factory was intimately connected with all that he did for housing. As we shall see, Bournville as an experiment in housing reform is not dependent on the factory. But the policy of raising wages and improving conditions of labour which is embodied in the factory, and the policy of improving the homes of the people which is embodied in the garden-city, do go very closely together.

It was in 1879 that the brothers Richard and George Cadbury resolved to take their Works out of the city into the country, and so moved out to a site between the villages of Selly Oak and King's Norton, some four miles away from the centre of Birmingham. The site was well chosen, because, apart from its natural amenities, the factory could be built within easy access to both railway and canal.

This move out into the district which later became Bournville gave room for the free development of ideas of factory organisation which had begun to germinate from the time when George Cadbury and his brother took over their father's business in Bridge Street in 1861. George Cadbury had hoped to be a doctor, and the desire to help suffering humanity which would have found an outlet in his profession was destined to shape his business policy. The family claims which pressed him into business, led him to consider the possibilities of the factory as an engine of social progress. From the beginning of his business career, he had broken with the old tradition of depressing wages. It was a cardinal principle of the Ricardian economics that wages and profits vary inversely. Profits would be high or low in proportion as wages were low or high. This doctrine justified the traditional policy of employers, who assumed that the natural way to increase profits is to cut wages. The same assumption underlies much popular socialist propaganda. George Cadbury, on the contrary, believed it to be an employer's first duty to pay a living wage, and if possible to raise wages progressively. He did not regard labour as an ordinary commodity to be bought as cheap as possible, and he was convinced that sound ethics would prove to be true economy. It is the employer's duty to look after the interests of his employees, and first and foremost to secure to them a fair return for their labour. By moving the factory out from the centre, the Cadburys were able to plan their buildings so as to secure the most favourable conditions of air and light. They were able to equip and organise their works on the most efficient lines. They also had room for providing all sorts of conveniences and amenities for their employees. It is not necessary to describe in detail the provision made for the welfare of the employees of Bournville. It runs from the provision of diningrooms, libraries, recreation rooms, swimming-baths and gymnasia, to extensive recreation grounds. It includes further, a medical and dental service, together with convalescent homes, the organisation

of all sorts of clubs, the provision of continued
education for employees under eighteen, and an
Education Department which responds to and
develops the varying demands for adult education.
There are also different forms of organisation to
encourage thrift, including a Pensions Scheme,
Housing Schemes and special facilities for employees to acquire ordinary shares in the business.
There is hardly an interest of any of the employees
which is not stimulated and catered for in some
way or other. In all this development, the firm
went ahead of legal requirements, and played the
part of pioneers. They abolished the system of
fines before it was legally forbidden, multiplied
safe-guards against accidents without waiting for
the pressure of Government inspectors. In sickness insurance and provision for old age, they
anticipated the subsequent developments of State
action, while in their Continuation School they
gave the lead which was embodied in the Fisher
Act, but not translated into reality. In these and
other ways, the factory was made the centre of a
healthy social life for those who worked in it, and
also a stimulus and a guide to public opinion and
State action.

When the works were moved out from Bridge
Street in '79, a few houses were built in the neighbourhood for some of the foremen employed in the
works, but it was not until 1895 that George
Cadbury acquired the larger part of the site of the
present Garden Village of Bournville, and entered
in earnest upon his career as a housing reformer.
In planning the village, George Cadbury aimed at

perserving as much as possible of the natural beauty of the site, particularly the trees. He wanted to attach an adequate garden to each house, for, as we have seen, he laid great stress on the value of a garden. He saw to it that each garden was provided with some fruit trees. The houses were built for the most part in pairs, and no two pairs were to be built to exactly the same design. Ample space was to be secured by not building more than eight houses to the acre. At first tenants could acquire the practical ownership of houses on a 999 years' lease, but later George Cadbury followed the policy of vesting the ownership of the land and the houses in a group of trustees. No individual derives any profit from Bournville. The site, and the bulk of the houses, are really held on trust for the nation, and any surplus from the rents, beyond the necessary cost of repair and the running expenses of the Trust, is to be used to finance further experiments in housing along similar lines. Bournville should thus be self-perpetuating, and self-propagating. It is necessary to point out that there is no such close connection between Bournville the Garden Village and the Works of Cadbury Brothers, as exists in some other garden cities that have been started by other firms. The houses in Bournville are not reserved, as is often supposed, for the employees in the factory, though probably nearly one half of the inhabitants of Bournville are actually employed in the factory. Nor does the continuance of Bournville depend on the continuance of the factory. If the factory were closed to-morrow,

Bournville as a contribution to the solution of the housing problem would continue. It is an independent attempt to show that real homes can be provided at a moderate rental.[1]

The factory and the village will always remain George Cadbury's outstanding achievements, but they by no means exhausted his interests. It must suffice to mention some of his other activities. He was a keen worker for Temperance; he took no small part in the movement for Old Age Pensions; he believed in the principle of collective bargaining and on more than one occasion gave public support to Trade Unions in times of industrial crisis, while he steadily advocated the principle of arbitration in industrial disputes; he was the personal friend of many Labour leaders and did not a little to promote the growth of the Labour party and to support Labour journalism; he threw his influence on the side of co-operation between Liberalism

[1] The name Bournville is now often applied not only to the original village lying between Raddlebarn Road and Mary Vale Road, but to the neighbouring sites in Hay Green and the Weoley Park Estate, which are now being developed by Public Utility Societies in line with the original trust. The secretary of the Bournville Village Trust has very kindly supplied me with the following details :—

" If you take the whole Estate, the total number of houses upon it, built or in course of construction, is 1807.

" Then, if a standard of $4\frac{1}{2}$ persons to each house is taken, we get an approximate total population of 8000.

"Then, about rents—older houses in the original village still come under the Rents Restriction Acts, that is to say, the rents are only 40 per cent. above pre-war, the lowest now being 8s. 9d. per week, which includes rates. Of the post-war houses built by the Trust in Hay Green Lane, the lowest rent is 12s. 6d. per week, which includes rates. These are comparable in accommodation."

and Labour; he was deeply concerned for the preservation of international peace and it was mainly in the hope of promoting this cause that he assumed large responsibilities in relation to the daily press. In every direction, the severely practical character of his judgments exposed him to charges of inconsistency. He regarded the extremes of wealth and poverty in modern society as indefensible, yet he was convinced that it was not a sound practical policy for Christian men to follow St Francis of Assisi.

"I have for many years given practically the whole of my income for charitable purposes, except what is spent upon my family, but this is not a satisfactory solution of the question. . . . Nearly all my money is invested in businesses in which I believe I can truly say the first thought is the welfare of the workpeople employed. Should Christian men sell all that they have, such businesses would probably come into the hands of unscrupulous men whose aim is to make dividends as large as possible, regardless of their workpeople." [1]

He believed gambling to be one of the greatest curses to our national life, yet when he found no paper could live without racing news, he did not withdraw from the press, and when it seemed that the last evening paper in London which remained loyal to Liberalism and the cause of peace was likely to be lost, he did not hesitate to incur the obloquy which the excellence of the betting tips in the *Star* brought upon him. In the same way, he blamed the out-and-out temperance reformers because of their habit of rejecting half-loaves, and,

[1] *Life*, p. 105.

while he faced all the odium attaching to the cause of Home Rule in Birmingham, he did not hesitate to support (in 1898) a Free Trade Liberal who was not a Home-Ruler, since he held that for the time the Home Rule question was in abeyance.

He had to face not only charges of inconsistency, but more abusive and unscrupulous criticism. When he gave £50 a week to support the Engineers during the lockout of 1897, he received the following anonymous postcard:

"£50 a week to the Engineers' Strikers"—splendid advertisement, sure to do your firm good; real ? charity.
"A Plymouth Brother."

Vanity Fair took him to task in a leading article:

"Mr George Cadbury is, no doubt, a well-meaning person; but is he a patriot ? Most sensible people will think not. With, of course, the best intentions in the world this gentleman is said to have guaranteed a subscription of £50 a week to the funds of the striking engineers; the subscription to be kept up until the masters make terms with the recalcitrant men. We can understand how the men are misled—how easily they may be misled—in spite of the old fable of the goose with the golden eggs; but Mr George Cadbury is a philanthropist, and philanthropists ought to know the difference between wholesome charity and the unwholesome maintenance of a mischievous quarrel. And if such a one did not perceive the difference, the Germans and Americans are at this very moment giving him what is called an ' object lesson ' in the matter. For these foreigners are playing their own game in subscribing to the strikers' funds. They know that by keeping up the strike they are bringing business to themselves. The German and the American hate us, but they love our money, and will get all they can of it. They know that every sovereign they send to the strikers will probably mean a reward to themselves of many pounds' worth of work. Mr George Cadbury has no such inducement to spend £50 a week; and why he should announce his intention of doing anything so foolish, so utterly unwholesome, and so wholly mischievous must pass the comprehension of every thinking man."

His action in financing the *Daily News* and the *Star* brought him, in addition to the high-toned denunciation of the *Spectator*, anonymous postcards with genial references to Chadband Cadbury.

It is, of course, open to anyone to question the wisdom of George Cadbury's action in either instance. But charges of cant and hypocrisy only recoil on the heads of those who make them. In these decisions, George Cadbury was absolutely free from self-advertisement or self-seeking. He came to them only after prayerful and careful thought. He did what he did, as being in his judgment the best he could do in the given situation. For himself he welcomed scoffing and abuse as some evidence that he was standing on the weaker side.

George Cadbury was the last man to claim any great significance for the reforms he accomplished and the first to recognise the importance of problems which lay beyond the range of his own undertakings. He hoped his work would stand as the work of a practical pioneer, but he knew he was but taking first steps. What then is the permanent worth of his deeds ?

We may freely concede that many and in some ways greater industrial problems still remain to be solved. George Cadbury described his relations

with his employees as paternal if not patriarchal.[1]
He valued this relationship because it was a
personal one and enabled him to carry his workers
with him as no purely business relationship would
have enabled him to do. Yet he felt that such
relationships became increasingly difficult as the
factory developed, and while such a control over
the lives of employees might be justified as a
transition-stage, paternalism was not a final ideal.
The conditions of co-operation and co-partnership
in industry have still to be worked out. George
Cadbury brought men to the margin of this promised land rather than led them into it. Then,
the development of the social side of the factory
might be criticised, and is criticised in some quarters,
on the ground that men and women thus find in
the factory the centre which they ought to find
in their community or even in their church. The
factory is thought to be stepping out of its sphere.
Perhaps the problem arises in particular in connection with education. Those who recognise
most gladly and fully the service of the Bournville
Works to continued education and higher adult
education, and who would not, as things are, have
the firm do anything less, may yet believe that
ideally all such educational enterprise should be
run by the community and detached from business

---

[1] It was characteristic of George Cadbury that in the early days
in Bridge Street, when the firm employed twenty persons, he
instituted the practice of gathering them together for family
worship—hymn, reading, prayer—at the beginning of each day.
He kept this practice up at Bournville until he was no longer
strong enough to conduct it. This family-worship was the key-
note of his relations with his employees.

undertakings. Yet others would criticise George Cadbury's achievements on the ground that they have been consummated within the limits of the present industrial system, that therefore they are but palliatives and, even worse, that they bolster up an essentially unjust commercialism.

By meeting the challenge of this last criticism, I can most easily bring out the value of George Cadbury's life-work. If the assumption of the need of more revolutionary change in industry be true, all that George Cadbury did, both in factory-organisation and in housing, will have to find its recognition and its place in any revolutionised industrial and social order. Unless, indeed, the factory-system itself is to be abandoned, all the arrangements for the health, welfare and comfort of the workers which George Cadbury introduced, must be retained and developed. If some features of the works at Bournville are to be taken over and discharged later on by the community, that will detract nothing from the honour due to George Cadbury. His contribution to housing will remain a perpetual reminder of the force of John Bright's definition of great statesmanship:

" The nation in every country dwells in the cottage : and unless the light of your Constitution can shine there, . . . rely upon it, you have yet to learn the duties of government."

Whatever the future may hold in the way of social revolution, any social revolution will stand condemned which cannot build on the work of George Cadbury.

But it may be that the demand for revolutionary change rests on a misunderstanding. It has been well pointed out by G. C. Field in his book on Guild Socialism that this demand assumes that the present state of things can be truly described as a system, whereas "the real feature of the present state of things is that there is no one system of industrial organisation, but that there is practically no limit to the different forms which have been or could be tried." The newer and morally more satisfying forms of industrial organisation will not be created by a revolutionary clearing of the site and by a rebuilding of our industrial machinery wholesale. They will come through the patient work of pioneers in individual firms. They will come through employers and labour leaders who realise that new occasions teach new duties. The lesson of George Cadbury's life as a manufacturer is that the life of the factory can be and should be reformed from within, and the work will be accomplished by men who

> . . . look in all their ends
> To God as judge and not their friends.

o

HENRY SCOTT HOLLAND

HENRY SCOTT HOLLAND (1848-1918)

By JAMES ADDERLEY, M.A.

HENRY SCOTT HOLLAND

HENRY SCOTT HOLLAND was the life and soul of the Christian Social Union. The Union was founded in 1890, and was merged into the Industrial Christian Fellowship after the War. Its place in religious social reformation comes between the original " Christian Socialists " and the modern promoters of C.O.P.E.C. Its distinctive character, which it owed to Henry Scott Holland, was that it was a Church of England Society and was designed to be, and in fact became, a rallying ground for definite Church members who, being persuaded of the duty of the Church in social and industrial matters, were anxious to know what they could do in solving immediate problems and to study economic principles in the light of their religion.

A leaflet,[1] issued in 1890 by Holland, expresses in a few words his own position. To understand it we must try to realise the common attitude of Christians generally towards the religious and economic questions of that time. It has been pointed out that there are four attitudes which Christians at different times in Church History have adopted in regard to economics.[2]

There is the ascetic idea that economic relations

---

[1] *The Ground of our Appeal*, C.S.U., 1890.
[2] See *Religion and the Rise of Capitalism*, by Tawney, pp. 16, 17.

belong to the sphere of unrighteousness, and that the Christian must escape from them if he can. There is the attitude of indifference which holds that religion has no concern with economic matters, and that Christians must go on their way in a state of complacent apathy while pocketing the dividends. Another is that which urges some particular revolutionary reform which will at once inaugurate the reign of righteousness. The last and most common and Christian way is to see in all human affairs, secular and sacred, the material out of which by patient study and faithful obedience to principle the Kingdom of God will eventually appear. This attitude is " seeking a synthesis of the external order and the religion of the spirit." Most Christians are coming round to this, and that it is so in the Church of England is largely due to Holland's work. There are very few now who would try to flee from the social problem into a desert ; there are scarcely any who now remain indifferent; not many who think there is a panacea for immediate application.

Holland's doctrine is a kind of Christian Fabianism. " The time has come to vote urgency for the social question," but it is of no use to hurry on reforms to which the collective conscience of the Church has not consented in principle.

This may sound a little belated, but we must remember that he is writing in the " eighties " of the last century. " We believe that political problems are rapidly giving place to the industrial problem, which, by its vastness, its variety, and its depth, must absorb our attention and our energy.

It is the intolerable situation into which the lower grades of our industrial population now find themselves driven that must force upon us a reconsideration of the economic principles and methods which have such disastrous and terrible results." We as Christians are convinced " that the ultimate solution of the social question is bound to be discovered in the Person and life of Christ. He is ' the Man ' and He must be the solution of all human problems."

Holland was for ever pleading that while the sympathy of Christ to the suffering poor had been faithfully preached, the thought of Him as a conquering King, overcoming the World, the living Lord and Master of the whole of human life, the " extension of the fruits of the Passion over the entire surface of human life " had been kept in the background of Church teaching. " The natural bonds which hold together men into societies and races must of necessity receive the new inflowing force which comes to them out of the supremacy of Him who gathers all men to Himself."

But to do this effectively is no easy matter. The problems raised are intricate. It cannot be said offhand what exactly the Lordship of Christ does demand of human society. How far can human society be expected to surrender itself to the dominion of Christ at any particular moment in history ? Holland felt that, while there was need for caution and study, the pace might well be considerably quickened. We must get past the merely sentimental assertion that " Christ is all in all " and see what that solemn truth precisely means in view of present facts. He appealed to his fellow Churchmen to get into contact with the experts in business and economics, and above all to allow themselves to be convinced that a way out must be discoverable if the doctrine of the Incarnation is true. We must seek the solution " in the unfaltering assertion of moral as supreme over mechanical laws."

This last sentence, which Holland kept repeating in different forms, drew down upon him the censure of critics from all sides, from politicians, commercial men and clergy alike. Yet it was only what Ruskin had said and what the chief political economist of the day, Professor Marshall, had himself declared to be in no way contrary to the findings of his own particular science.

In his books Marshall had written : " An economic law is a statement that a certain course of action may be expected under certain conditions from the members of an industrial group : and that action is the normal action of the members of that group. It is not the function of any science to lay down practical precepts or to prescribe rules of life. Economic laws are merely statements of tendencies expressed in the indicative mood, and not ethical precepts in the imperative. Economics deal with the class of motives that are measurable only." He went further, and frankly accused the " hangers on of the Science who had no reverence for it, and used it simply as an engine for keeping the working classes in order." " Public opinion, based on sound economics and just morality will, it may be hoped, become ever more and more the arbiter of the conditions of industry." [1]

It was the task of Holland to bring this home to his fellow Christians, who still retained the timidity of those who had lived in the earlier part of the nineteenth century and talked of " iron laws." In his preface to Mr Richmond's lectures on "Economic Morals," [2] which were the introduction to the whole movement of the Christian Social Union, Holland writes in his characteristic way :

" We live as shuttlecocks bandied about between our political economy and our Christian morality. We go to a certain distance with the science, and then when things get ugly and squeeze we suddenly introduce moral considerations and human kindness and charity. And then, again, this seems weak and we pull up short and go back to tough economic principle. So we live in miserable double-mindedness. Each counter-motive intervenes at purely arbitrary points. When our economy is caught in a tangle we fly off to our morality. When our morality lands us in a social problem we take refuge in some economic law. There is no consistency in our treatment of facts : no harmony in our inward convictions."

We dwell on this because it is here that we find the source of the practical result of much of Holland's teaching. We have only to compare the pro-

----

[1] See *Economics of Industry*. Preface, p. 411 and elsewhere. Also *Principles of Economics*. Preface, p. v (1st edition) (Macmillan).

[2] See *Henry Scott Holland*, edited by Stephen Paget, p. 172 (John Murray).

gressive utterances of the Lambeth Conferences to see how steadily Christian economic thought was advancing. In 1888 the Archbishop declared that " no more important problems can well occupy the attention whether of clergy or laity than such as are connected with what is popularly known as Socialism." During the following decade Holland and his Union were clamouring that the Christian Church must have a mind of its own, loyal to its Master whatever the world may say. By 1897 the Lambeth Bishops had adopted almost word for word Holland's pamphlet and waxed bolder, announcing that " a Christian community as a whole is responsible morally for the character of its own economic and social order and for deciding to what extent matters affecting that order are to be left to individual initiative and to the unregulated play of economic forces." When the Christian Social Union met at Holborn Town Hall to plead for a " living wage " for all in the name of Christ, Holland was laughed at for his speech, but in 1908 the Lambeth fathers were prepared to say that " The fundamental Christian principle of the remuneration of labour is that the first charge upon any industry must be the maintenance of the labourer—an idea which it has been sought to express in popular language by the phrase ' a living wage.' "

Thus Holland came into his own, and his passionate appeals, ridiculed and torn to bits by criticism, have now become the commonplaces of almost every ruridecanal conference in the country.

We can only give samples of his utterances. For

thirty years or more he was preaching at St Paul's, lecturing in all parts of the country, publishing sermons, heading deputations to the Government, advising young men and women, studying minutely all the details of women's work, the sweating system and industrial diseases.

There was never a strike but Holland knew almost at the beginning exactly what had led to it and the particular points to be considered on both sides. Nobody was ever more fair towards contending parties and no one more anxious to bring peace without any compromise of truth or justice. As early as 1889, during the great Dock Strike, he compiled a letter to the *Times*, in which, in a startling phrase, he described the casuals who went into work at 3d. an hour as the " Esaus of modern industry," selling their freedom for a miserable wage.

Besides the fundamental question of how far economic law is law in the sense that it is inexorable like the law of gravitation, Holland had much to say about the objections to State interference, in his day more violently opposed than it is now.

Here, again, he put his finger on the point which was really at issue. Does the State mean now what it meant in the days when its interference was so much criticised ? The case for interference has never been more vividly and humorously put than in his famous article, " Every man his own Grandmother," first published in *Goodwill*, a Parish Magazine which for many years attempted month by month to interest ordinary church folk in social problems.[1] At the risk of spoiling it by short

[1] See *Scott Holland's Goodwill*, p. 52 (Wells Gardner & Co.).

extracts we cannot forbear to give some because the article is especially characteristic of Holland's style and really had an effect on the attitude of the Church. " Grandmotherly Legislation," he begins. " There is no taunt more familiar or more crushing than that. Whenever we have been sickened by some terrible carelessness which leaves workers to be poisoned by white lead, or mangled by unguarded machines, or stifled by lack of ventilation and we can stand it no longer . . . and devise excellent and careful bills against these disasters : then there breaks out the old cry which has always haunted us—Where is the old sturdy independence of the British artisan ? Why this coddling and meddling and fussing as if he were a big baby ? You will ruin his moral vigour by all this grandmotherly legislation. . . . We tremble ! Yet, need we collapse so ignominiously ? The truth is that the old taunt is obsolete ; it has outlived its day.

" Let us see how this is.

" And first let us pluck up heart in defence of our grandmothers. . . . Why should all legislation be bad because it is a grandmother's ? Why has a grandmother's wisdom been entirely confined to the humble and limited sphere of sucking eggs ?

" In that subtle art she is acknowledged by the universal consent of mankind to be supreme : she has nothing to learn there. . . . Still, if so skilled at this point, why should she be a byword in all other departments ?

" The sting of the taunt lies in the suggestion that this safeguarding legislation, which is in question, represents something done for someone by somebody else. It implies that you have to be looked after by a nurse from outside, from above, who will see that your hair is combed and your hands are washed. . . . Why run to her to do for you that which you ought to do for yourself ? That is the imputation, and against it I would retort that it is hopelessly out of date. For it starts with the presupposition that all legislation must come down on the people from above, that to make laws is to invoke the aid of an outsider. Once of course this was true. The laws made on behalf of the industrial class . . . were the efforts of benevolent and philanthropic on-lookers, exercising a paternal interest over those under their charge. But all this has long ago been changed. Legislation is now made by the people for themselves. . . . They themselves pass the laws, not their grandmothers for them. Such legislation proceeds out of your own rational self-control. Your reason determines it. You are nursing your-self : you are grandmothering yourself. . . . It is simply an expression of the general public conscience . . . the workman who is protected against risk is protecting himself. . . . The whole act proceeds without the ghost of a grandmother appearing on the scene. The good old girl has withdrawn to the privacy in which she dedicates herself to perfecting her traditional skill in the matter of eggs. It is the man now who is handling his own destiny not in the spirit of an ' old woman ' making a fuss, but of one who is seriously bent on the task of bringing into life the order and shapeliness and security and leisure which it so terribly lacks."

Holland pursued this line of thought in a chapter

of *Good Citizenship*, a book of essays by prominent " Christian Socialists," in which he maintained that " Law fastens its obligations upon us from within as well as from without. The State which imposes the Law is our social self : and in obeying the Law we obey ourself."

" Our keenest hopes for the realisation of Socialistic ideals are turning more and more in the direction of some process by which the growing sense of human solidarity should inspire and mould the body of Law and fill it with the soul of fellowship and love. Such a process would be gradual, manifold, immense : and would therefore be adequate to the scale and complexity of civilised life. In the face of this complexity, Socialist programmes are apt to look childish and crude. They too obviously omit at least half of what human nature has now grown to be. They collapse into the dreary flatitude of Mr Bellamy's *Looking Backward*, or else, while preserving the imaginative and romantic elements which he forgot, they boldly propose, with Mr Morris, to reduce life to its early simplicities. Yet any attempt to roll back man's history is doomed to the transitoriness and the impotence which are the stamp of all reactions." [1]

Holland accordingly was never a dreamer nor a proposer of wild-cat schemes. He went to the heart of problems such as those of women's work and factory labour, found out by patient inquiry what exactly was happening and asked the experts what could conceivably be done at once and what

[1] *Good Citizenship*, edited by J. E. Hand, p. 304 (George Allen).

could not. Behind the experts he stood, cheering them on by his inexhaustible faith and hope, giving their demands a human and even a poetical voice, insisting on firm principle and high morality in settling the minutest details of what they might ask for and what they might work for. Armed with all this he would head deputations to the Home Office and make speeches on platforms, and month by month report to the Church in the pages of the *Commonwealth* how far they had progressed.

It must not be thought that Holland only busied himself about wages and hours. To him the " social question " included everything that had to do with human society, whether in an industrial class or in the nation at large or in the world-wide comity of nations. He worried himself continually about the colour question, the opium traffic, the name of England in foreign countries, the treaties we had put our signature to and had not honoured, the troubles of persecuted Christians in Armenia and Macedonia, and a hundred other matters of the kind. He gave a fresh impetus to missionary work. No one could hold an audience at a missionary meeting as he did. The broad questions surrounding every Mission field which he handled so vigorously gave a new interest to the audiences whose minds hovered between a sort of inherited distrust of Missions and a wonder if they could get away from the meeting at the expense of a threepenny bit.

Holland's great heart went out to all the victims of the callous law of the survival of the fittest, whether black or white, in Africa and India, or in the mills and factories of the midlands and the north.

It seemed to him that the whole Christian community should unite and come to the rescue of those who were suffering from conditions which were utterly unworthy of a civilisation that called itself Christian. He felt this also very strongly in regard to commercial morality and the temptations to which young Christians were subjected in places of business to tell lies or to starve. He worked hard with Rev. John Carter, the Secretary of the C.S.U., in investigating the " sins of trade," such as illicit commissions, adulteration, sweated labour, etc., and produced " White Lists " in many towns so that conscientious consumers should know with whom they might safely deal. The sense of responsibility in Christian shareholders and consumers is very much stronger in Church people now and this is owing to a great extent to the work of Holland. Christian social reform was no " extra," as he would say, like " dancing or drawing in a girls' school." It was of the very essence of religion and especially of Churchmanship. If he were asked why the Church had taken so long to wake up to the urgency of this, he would reply that until of late in this country there had been practically no Church to wake up. The Labour Movement and the Church Movement had gone on independently, each fully occupied in finding for itself a place in the sun. The Industrial Revolution had caught the Church napping. The Methodist and Evangelical Movements had no corporate message to the nation, nor would the nation have listened if they had had one. It is extremely difficult for a Church to have a collective policy at all far ahead of the nation, at large. Individual Christians take their economic views from the average opinions and policies accepted by the bulk of their contemporaries. Holland would never agree that to make a man a Christian immediately guaranteed that he would become a social reformer. It all depended on the level which the whole body of Christians had at the time reached. Individual Christians would not advance by themselves to any social revolution. They would just stand still at the point at which the main body were encamped. Unless they have a strong corporate opinion at their backs their religion tends to be of an individualistic character, they occupy themselves with private acts of piety and charity, and if they go further afield, it is generally in the direction of "foreign missions," sufficiently removed from the social life of home to prevent them from being thought revolutionists. Thus it was that while the earlier religious movements produced great saints they had little of what Mr and Mrs Hammond call "social sense." [1] They could contemplate the most appalling injustice and the most miserable conditions of life and labour all around them without feeling that Christianity called for drastic social reform. The Christian Socialists of the days of Maurice and Kingsley were a very small body and their sphere of activity was limited. They were prophets rather than social reformers. Holland and his friends may be said to have carried the whole movement on to another

[1] See *The Town Labourer*, by J. L. and B. Hammond. Chapters on "The Conscience of the Rich" and "The Religion of the Poor" (Longmans).

P

stage. It was in the new movement that, as has been said, the "honey" of Maurice "passed into the ritualistic hive." "The influence," says Mr Charles Masterman (of Maurice), "has been almost entirely in the strengthening of a movement in the Church whose leaders he fought unwearyingly for nearly half a century."[1] For it was the Tractarian Movement that in its later form combined the "Catholic Church" of Pusey with the "Kingdom of Christ" of Maurice and produced the new Christian Socialism of which Holland was the prophet and chief.

If the Labour Movement revolutionised the condition of the poor, the Tractarian Movement revolutionised the condition of the Church of England, and, to a great extent, of English Christianity as a whole. But before the Church could enter into the economic arena as a united force it had to realise itself as a body. There was no corporate institution believing sufficiently in itself or able to speak with one voice, there was no Church able to inspire whole groups of its members to take part in the reform of society. The whole of the first part of the Tractarian Movement was occupied in putting life into the Church as an institution. The Church re-read its Prayer-Book, inspected its spiritual title-deeds, rehearsed its creeds, restored its sanctuaries, beautified its services and its ritual. All this was very difficult to do. More especially was it so because the members of the Church were at loggerheads with one another as to how it was best to be done. Added to this confusion, there was

---

[1] *Frederick Denison Maurice*, by C. F. G. Masterman, p. 5 (Mowbray).

a tradition in the Church, the same tradition as that of the wealthy classes who had captured the institution, and that tradition was intensely conservative, averse to any political or social change. This too had got to be broken into and at least partially dispersed before the Church as a body could occupy itself corporately with social reform. If we turn to Labour we find a similar kind of preoccupation. It could not act corporately, for it was actually illegal to do so. If the Church was trying to get its members to use their ancient liberty to act together, Labour was bent on getting leave of the legislature to do the same thing. Few people who now talk of the freedom of Trade Unions realise that it was only in the " eighties " of the last century that the remaining combination laws were repealed. Labour was struggling for its life. There were individual Christians in the Labour movement whose religion was the basis of their work, but, as Kingsley saw, it was impossible for the masses to think of religion. What Arnold Toynbee described as " a population huddled together in towns in filthy dens like wild animals, women working like beasts in mines, countrymen famished in dark hovels, tumult and anger among the people," was hardly a soil on which Churchmanship could be expected to grow. What then brought the Church and Labour together ? It was the need which each felt for the other when the corporate position of each had been sufficiently secured for them to feel at all.

Organisation of the Church on one side and of Labour on the other began to bear its fruit.

Now, Holland was in the forefront in all the

movements that brought them together, whether by East London Settlements such as the Oxford House or the Eton Mission, or by the activities of the Christian Social Union. He felt, with many other great men at the time, in Nonconformist circles, in Parliament and in society generally, that it is almost impossible with any great effect to make the Gospel of Christ known and believed where the conditions of life and labour are such that material satisfaction must be the primary object of men's thoughts. Nothing irritated Holland more than the taunt that the Christian Socialists were doing " unspiritual " work. It was precisely the contrary. They were more concerned about the soul of Dives than the sores of Lazarus. They were out for justice and brotherhood ; they believed that only Christ could reform society, and that it was not by mere individual conversion of pious persons, but rather by the uplifting of a new ideal for Christ's Church.

Just at the same time Labour, having secured its organisation and thirsting to realise its aspirations, was also making the discovery that materialism (and what the nineteenth century called " progress ") were eminently unsatisfactory. The " militant atheism " of Mr Bradlaugh was giving way before the moral enthusiasm of Blatchford and the *Clarion*. The new socialism was largely in the hands of local preachers, especially in the north. Men of a robust religion like Mr Keir Hardie were the newest of the pioneers. The atheism of the Continental socialists was almost unknown among their British comrades. Holland, it should be said, was a Liberal in politics, devoted to his friend, Mr Gladstone : and while he had great sympathy with the Socialists and admired what he called their " moral zeal," he never joined the Labour Party, which he thought by its recklessness tended to drive the nation back into the " toughest tyranny of private property " ever known. He was content to confine himself to the task of converting the Anglican Church. The principles of his Union, as set out officially, were as follows :—

1. To claim for the Christian Law the ultimate authority to rule Christian practice.

2. To study in common how to apply the moral truths and principles of Christianity to the social and economic difficulties of the present time.

3. To present Christ in practical life as the living Master and King, the enemy of wrong and selfishness, the power of righteousness and love.

It may be well now to explain why the Christian Social Union was confined to members of the Anglican communion.

Holland was an Anglican of the Anglicans, and he felt that it was of the utmost importance to convert his own fellow-churchmen, as churchmen, to the new way of regarding their responsibilities. It seemed sometimes narrow-minded to keep out the Nonconformists, but Holland was probably right. Nobody more thoroughly appreciated the efforts of the Free Churches in social reform, but he also felt that such a revolution of thought, as it was for many Christians, must proceed from the deepest convictions of their personal religion. He did not want to disturb the movement by bringing in questions of heresy or schism to confuse the issue. He would have done a good work if he had made every Anglican, just because he was an Anglican, recognise that he must be a social reformer. The Church services, especially the Holy Communion, the creeds and the prayers, the parishes and the old parish Churches and Cathedrals, the title of "National Church," all expressed what to him were great realities full of meaning in the Christian social direction.

It was as much as he could hope to do in a lifetime to bring this home to the Church of England. For this he laboured literally night and day. With a wealth of language, original and poetical, he preached innumerable sermons, made innumerable speeches, published hundreds of articles in his own little paper, *The Commonwealth*. They must be read to be appreciated. Unfortunately he never published any one great book but the volumes of sermons, and the back numbers of his paper can still be read and with wonderful freshness. His abundant humour, which to most of us was his great charm, was to some a stumbling-block. They could not see the psychological value of it. They had an idea that he was not serious. Perhaps some of them felt sure he was right but preferred to discount his message lest it should make them uncomfortable.

He has never been appreciated except by a few of his intimate friends. The public still (if it remembers him at all) just laughs at his jokes and sighs that he can no longer amuse us. Yet one of his contemporaries has said publicly that his was one of the four greatest minds of the nineteenth century.

He was intensely religious and profoundly theological, yet never for one moment out of touch with the realities of modern life. He might appear at one time as harping on one string, the Divinity of Christ or the necessity of Grace. But no one believed more thoroughly in the Humanity of Jesus. None ever more thoroughly extracted the honey from the Gospel stories. He could make our Lord's parables speak without any vulgar realism.[1] You sat on the seashore of Galilee and found yourself in Pall Mall without any obvious scene-shifting. He dealt with the soul of society as with the soul of an individual. He had the faith of a Maurice in the presence of God in human history and the utter self-abandonment to the reality of the Father in the sunshine of which St Francis basked. He could no more fancy God outside politics or art or games than he could imagine a day without the sun. Instinctively his Christianity leapt out at every fresh crisis to deal with the situation. Attitudes and platitudes were to him the twin brothers of faithlessness and despair. To have no vision was to let the people perish. To say that things were impossible because " human nature could not be changed," was to Holland more than a policy of despair ; it was to act the part of a defeatist in the Holy War and to deny the Redeemer Christ. It was to stop praying and to throw the Bible, the Church and the Sacraments on the dust heap. Nineteenth century materialism had no terrors for him. He foresaw the time when it would have no friends. It was this Christian vitalism which kept Church people alive through

[1] See especially *God's City* (Longmans).

many dark days. No man ever had more faith in orthodox religion or hope for the world when it should come round to it. He defends the Creed because he is sure that it is the only basis of true progress. Theology could never be dull and dry nor apart from life for him. Modern heresies must be stripped bare and their inadequacy and futility exposed, not because he wants to prop up a failing Church, but for precisely the opposite reason, to show that the Church is winning all along the line. He does not apologise for the Church. He politely intimates to the heretics that they are labouring under a delusion as to what Christianity means and for what the Church is out. One is munching the old bones of controversies which have long since lost their meaning : another so called new theologian has gone back to pre-Christian times.

Faith, Hope and Love and the old Creed are after all the best offensive and defensive. An agnostic once went to Holland to have an argument.

He began—" Of course I am a pessimist." "Oh," said Holland, "then don't let's talk about Christianity. Let's have tea."

JAMES KEIR HARDIE

JAMES KEIR HARDIE (1856–1915)

By A. FENNER BROCKWAY

JAMES KEIR HARDIE

THE significance of the life and work of James Keir Hardie is not yet realised. His memory is revered in the Labour movement as the Church reveres the memory of its saints, but in the mind of the public Hardie is still too often regarded as a destructive rather than constructive force. History will measure him differently. More than any other man he was the creator of the modern British Labour movement, which is undeniably one of the great formative influences of the time. Its founder, therefore, cannot fail to stand out in history as a figure of exceptional significance.

Thirty-five years ago there was no independent political Labour movement in this country. When Hardie first advocated its establishment, he was denounced not only by the spokesmen of wealth but with equal vigour by the representatives of the workers. Yet within this short period the movement which Hardie initiated has already been responsible for the government of Britain. Rarely has the work of a pioneer reaped its reward more rapidly. No serious student of the developments of our time can therefore be indifferent to the experiences and outlook of the man in whose vision and activity this movement had its birth.

Hardie was born in a one-roomed cottage in the

mining village of Legbrannock in Lanarkshire in 1856. His father was not a miner, however, but a ship's carpenter, and it was in the shipbuilding district of Glasgow that we find Hardie in his early boyhood. His home knew intense poverty. Employment was irregular, and when an accident incapacitated his father for several weeks—there were no unemployment allowances and workmen's compensation then—all the hard-won savings went and debts mounted up. It was in this hard environment that Hardie grew up.

One of his early memories was a strike. Before it ended most of the household goods had been sold and the needs of the home were so acute that it was necessary for Hardie—only seven years old— to go out to work. He had intended to become apprenticed as a brass-finisher, but, when it was found that that meant a year's work without wages, he became a message boy at half-a-crown a week instead. His parents tried to compensate for his withdrawal from school by teaching him to read in the evenings. Hardie often said that his love of reading began from these days, and spoke with tender gratitude of the care with which his mother and father taught him.

These child-time experiences made a deep impression. All through his life, Hardie felt bitterly the injustice of denying to children the right to enjoy their childhood. The most bitter of these memories he has described. The Clyde shipworkers had been locked out. His slender wage was the only income of the family. Everything in the home which could be turned into food had been sold. One child had died ; another was about to be born.

" The outlook was black," wrote Hardie long afterwards, " but there was worse to come, and the form it took made it not only a turning-point in my life, but also in my outlook upon men and things. I had reached an age at which I understood the tragedy of poverty, and had a sense of responsibility to those at home far beyond my years. I knew that, despite the brave way in which my mother was facing the situation, she was feeling the burden almost too great for her to bear, and on more than one occasion I had caught her crying by herself.

" One winter morning I turned up late at the baker's shop where I was employed, and was told I had to go upstairs to see the master. I was kept waiting outside the door of the dining-room while he said grace—he was noted for religious zeal—and, on being admitted, found the master and his family seated round a large table. He was serving out bacon and eggs while his wife was pouring coffee from a glass infuser, which at once—shamefaced and terrified as I was—attracted my attention. I had never before seen such a beautiful room, nor such a table, loaded as it was with food and beautiful things.

" The master read me a lecture before the assembled family on the sin of slothfulness, and added that, though he would forgive me for that once, if I sinned again by being late I should be instantly dismissed ; and so sent me to begin work.

" But the injustice of the thing was burning hot within me, all the more that I could not explain why I was late. The fact was that I had not yet tasted food. I had been up most of the night tending my ailing brother, and had risen betimes in the morning, but had been made late by assisting my mother in various ways before starting. The work itself was heavy and lasted from seven in the morning till closing time.

" Two mornings later, a Friday, I was again a few

minutes late, from the same source, and was informed on arriving at the shop that I was discharged and my fortnight's wages forfeited by way of punishment. The news stupefied me, and finally I burst out crying and begged the shopwoman to intercede with the master for me. The morning was wet and I had been drenched in getting to the shop and must have presented a pitiable sight as I stood at the counter in my wet patched clothes. She spoke with the master through a speaking tube, presumably to the breakfast room I remembered so well, but he was obdurate, and finally she, out of the goodness of her heart, gave me a piece of bread and advised me to look for another place.

" For a time I wandered about the streets in the rain, ashamed to go home where there was neither food nor fire, and actually discussing whether the best thing was not to go and throw myself in the Clyde and be done with a life that had so little attractions. In the end I went to the shop and saw the master and explained why I had been late. But it was all in vain. The wages were never paid. But the master continued to be a pillar of the Church and a leading light in the religious life of the city."

Hardie, as we shall see later, was big enough to distinguish between religion and the actions of some of those who claim its inspiration; but this incident indicates why many who feel social injustice intensely sometimes become hostile to religion.

Indeed, it had this effect for a time in Hardie's home. His parents had had a strict religious upbringing and had encouraged their children to attend Sunday School. This experience made them free-thinkers, and the works of Paine and Ingersoll shared the shelves with the Bible and Bunyan.

Unemployment drove Hardie's father to sea

once more for a period, and the mother and family
settled down in Newarthill, a mining village.
Hardie, now ten, went down the pit. His work
was to open and close a door which kept the air
supply in the right direction. For ten hours each
day he stood at his post, alone in the darkness—a
cruel job for a boy who ought to have been playing
in the fields and learning in the school-room.

Hardie still eagerly sought knowledge, however,
and went each evening to a night school. His
mother gave him every encouragement, and, as he
grew into his teens, at her instigation he mastered
shorthand, with the object of becoming a journalist.
Events soon proved the wisdom of this preparation
for an alternative occupation to that provided by
the mine.

Hardie's reading and his natural idealism led him,
as he grew into young manhood, to appreciate,
anew, the beauty and truths of the teachings of
Christianity. Whilst still rejecting what he regarded as the doctrinal accretions of the Church,
and scorning the shams of many of its adherents,
he identified himself with what seemed to him to
be the simplest organised expression of Christianity,
the Evangelical Union. He also became an enthusiastic temperance reformer, and it was as such that
he began his public life. His platform experience
in this connection led his fellow-miners to appoint
him chairman at their meetings. Some of his
church and temperance friends warned him against
becoming a Labour agitator, but he had no use for
a Christianity which did not protest against social
wrongs. Miners' wages were then down to 1s. 8d.

and 2s. a day, and Hardie was impatient with a religion " which looked only to a heaven in the next world and ignored the hell in this."

Hardie's courageous championship of his fellows soon led to conflict with the management. One morning the manager of his pit—the family had moved to Hamilton on Hardie's father's obtaining work in the neighbourhood—told him peremptorily to get off the company's grounds. " We'll hae nae damned Hardies in this pit," he said, and he carried out his threat by dismissing the two younger brothers as well. This action made Hardie the recognised leader of the men. He got a living by opening a shop with his mother, and began journalism in a small way by acting as local correspondent to the *Glasgow Weekly Mail*. But his chief interest lay in the organisation of the miners. At twenty-three he was appointed their Scottish secretary.

I need not describe in detail Hardie's activity at this period, though it was strenuous and exciting. A ten weeks' strike temporarily smashed the men's organisation, and Hardie settled down at Cumnock, with his young wife—whom he had first met in his temperance work—and devoted himself to journalism. The pastor of the church which Hardie attended asked him to write some notes for the *Cumnock News*, whilst he was away. The pastor did not return, and Hardie was invited to join the staff.

The *Cumnock News* was a Liberal paper, and Hardie was soon drawn into the struggle for a more democratic franchise. He joined the Liberal

Association and became prominent at its local meetings. At the same time he carried on his temperance work, and was also active at his church, preaching at the street corners and occupying the pulpit on occasions. He read incessantly. Carlyle, Ruskin and Emerson, and, above all, Robert Burns, were his favourite authors.

The extension of the franchise in 1884 led Hardie to turn his mind to the possibility of returning Labour representatives to Parliament. He converted the *Miner*, a weekly paper which he had started in 1887, from " a Journal for Underground Workers " to " an Advanced Political Journal." He carried on his propaganda with a fervent evangelical zeal. " The world to-day is sick and weary at heart," he wrote. " Even our clergy are for the most part dumb dogs who dare not bark. So it was in the days of Christ. They who proclaimed a God-given gospel to the world were the poor and the comparatively unlettered. We need to-day a return to the principles of the Gospel which, by proclaiming all men sons of God and brethren one with another, makes it impossible for one, Shylock-like, to insist on his rights at the expense of another."

At first Hardie was ready that the workers should seek political expression through the Liberal Party. He was not yet a Socialist, and only insisted that the organised workers should have a voice in the selection of the candidates who sought to represent them. The test came when a vacancy occurred in Mid-Lanark in 1888. At the request of the miners, Hardie offered himself to the Liberal Association as candidate. The Liberal Executive

Q

chose a young Welsh lawyer, and Hardie stood as an independent Labour candidate.

Hardie was, of course, badly defeated, but this election was a turning-point in the political development of Labuor. It convinced Hardie of the impossibility of a Labour Party within the Liberal Party. Within three months the Scottish Labour Party was established, with Hardie as its secretary. Whilst not avowedly Socialist, its programme included the nationalisation of transport and banking.

Hardie then began the task of converting the British Trade Union movement to a belief in the necessity for independent political action. At the Bradford Trades Union Congress the same year he led the demand. The officials of the Congress were mostly Liberal politicians, and his criticism of the inadequacy of the Liberal Party was held to be a personal attack upon them. He was regarded as disloyal, impossible and revolutionary, much as a Communist is regarded in official Labour circles to-day. Yet within ten years the Trades Union Congress had accepted the view of this fanatical young miner, and had decided to form the Labour Party.

It was at this time, too, that Hardie began his contacts with the Labour movement abroad. At the Bradford Conference we find him presiding over an informal meeting of French and British delegates, and in the following November he attended a conference of European Trade Union representatives. He was much impressed by the zeal of the delegates from abroad—" Socialists to a man "—and in his description of the conference for the first time, I think, announced his adherence to Socialism. " Socialism is in the ascendant and everybody knows it," he wrote. " The marching order has been given, and it is ' Forward ' ! Henceforth there can be no alienation between British and Continental workers."

But if Hardie discovered his Socialism in this meeting with Socialists from the Continent, he interpreted it in a very different way from them. Continental Socialism was hard, dogmatic and materialistic. Hardie was tender, broad and idealistic. There already existed in Britain two Socialist organisations—the Social Democratic Federation, embodying much of the Continental outlook and spirit, and the Fabian Society, academical and wedded to the method of permeation. Neither had contact with the workers' movement. Hardie's great contribution was to express Socialism in generous, human terms, and to identify it with the actual life and struggle of the workers. It was because the Independent Labour Party, which he formed in 1893, embodied this spirit and policy that it succeeded where previous Socialist organisations failed.

How was it that British Socialism developed on these lines ? More than one factor was responsible, but, so far as Keir Hardie influenced it, I think it can be said that his religious idealism determined the tone of his expression of Socialism. " Socialism," he said repeatedly, " is a great *moral* movement. I am a Socialist because Socialism means Fraternity founded on Justice, and the fact that, in order to secure this, certain economic changes are necessary is a mere incident in our great human crusade. My protest is against economics being considered the whole of Socialism, or even the vital part of it."

But before the Independent Labour Party was formed Hardie had returned to Parliament. A Committee of Socialists and Radicals, dissatisfied with the old Parties, invited him to contest a bye-election in West Ham in 1892. The Liberal candidate died suddenly on the eve of the contest, and Hardie was victorious in a straight issue with the Conservatives. His entry to the House of Commons in a tweed jacket and cloth cap caused an extraordinary sensation. There was no bravado about this : Hardie wore the clothes to which he was accustomed and in which he was most comfortable. The Press denounced Hardie's action as an affront to the decency and respectability of Parliament. Perhaps sub-consciously they realised that the workman's clothes heralded the end of the domination of wealth in the affairs of the nation.

Meanwhile, the Independent Labour Party was being formed. Following upon the establishment of the Scottish Labour Party in 1888, similar organisations were being set up in various parts of England. In January, 1893, their representatives met in Bradford and inaugurated the Independent Labour Party. It started its work in a heroic spirit. A bye-election was no sooner announced than Hardie or one of his equally zealous comrades appeared on the scene. It mattered not whether

there was a branch of the Party or not.   A few
faithful souls were gathered together in some small
room, watches and dinner-sets were pawned to
enable the first handbills to be printed, and the
campaign began.   The candidate only polled a few
hundred votes.   What did it matter ?   Educational work had been done.   New converts had
been won.   The new idea was growing.

In the General Election of 1895 twenty-nine
Independent Labour Party candidates were nomin-
ated.   Every one, including Hardie, was defeated !
There was not the slightest sign of dejection.
Had not their candidates averaged a vote of 1592,
compared with the few hundreds they had learned
to expect ?

I need not describe Hardie's further work in
detail.   These were the decisive years.   Partly
because of the religious earnestness of the Inde-
pendent Labour Party pioneers, partly because of
the folly of their opponents, the idea for which
Hardie stood had captured the Trade Union movement by the end of the century.   In 1900 the
Labour Representation Committee, with Ramsay
MacDonald as its first secretary, was established.
It was a federation of Trade Unions and Socialist
organisations, such as the Independent Labour
Party.   In the General Election of 1906 thirty
Labour members were returned to the House of
Commons.   Eighteen years later the Labour Party
had grown so powerful that it became responsible
for the government of the country.

Hardie did not live to see the Labour Party
definitely adopt Socialism as its objective.   This

development, crowning his work, took place three years after his death. Some Socialists, like the Social Democratic Federation, were not prepared to affiliate to the Labour Party until it definitely avowed Socialism. That was not the way of Hardie and the Independent Labour Party. Hardie saw that the emancipation of the workers must come through the workers' movement. He was prepared to serve and wait, confident that the educational activity of the Independent Labour Party within the Party and the experience of political and economic development would in time lead the Labour movement to a realisation that its purpose must be not merely to win better conditions within the existing system of society, but to build a better system, in which class division and poverty would be ended. Hardie's faith has been amply justified.

Hardie's Socialism was as broad as humanity. He did not merely champion the workers against oppression. Wherever there was oppression he identified himself with those struggling against it. He understood the wider significance of the Woman Suffrage movement and, in the face of much misunderstanding, espoused their cause, and even refrained from criticism when some of the militants attacked him, though this hurt him deeply. He was the friend of every subject race asserting its right to liberty, and won the affection and trust of the Indian, Egyptian, and negro peoples as few British men have done. Freedom and Brotherhood were his two watchwords. He loved children and animals. He made a practice of noting in his diary the birthdays of the children in the working-class homes in which he stayed during his visits about the country, and even when he was in the far parts of the world never forgot to send them birthday cards. He was the friend of the pit pony no less than of the pitman, and raised his voice in Parliament again and again to protest against the cruelties which mankind imposed upon their brothers of the field and forest.

Hardie was, of course, an uncompromising opponent of militarism and war. In the height of jingo passion he faced danger unflinchingly during the Boer War to utter his denunciation of what he regarded as a barbarous crime against another people. In the International Socialist movement he pleaded again and again that the workers should refuse to murder each other in war. When the Great War occurred, his disappointment at the failure of the Labour movement to resist it internationally was intense. I was present at the first meeting of the National Council of the Independent Labour Party after war had been declared. Hardie was a broken man. " I cannot fight this War like I fought the Boer war," he said wearily. " I haven't the strength in me. I must leave it to you younger men."

It was the first time I had ever seen Hardie dejected and defeated. His biggest hopes had been shattered. But he was better than his word. In Parliament and the country he courageously raised his voice on behalf of International Brotherhood. As the slaughter went on, however, he suffered more and more acutely. The tragedy of it killed him. A little more than a year after the declaration of war he passed away, crushed by the ever-present thought of the suffering and sorrow around him, despairing in the failure of the Labour movement to be true to its internationalism.

Like all great creative personalities, Hardie found the inspiration of his life in the deeper things of the spirit. Even when overwhelmed with immediate duties, he would find some secluded and beautiful spot where alone he could refresh his soul by communion with the universal life which he was seeking to express. He was always conscious of a Divine Purpose, and he revered, above all, the life and teachings of Christ, who lived it so completely.

Towards the end of his life he said that were he to live it again he would devote it to the advocacy of the Gospel of Christ. Perhaps this avowal was due to a sense of the failure of the Labour movement when faced by the crisis of the War, though he was conscious of the equal failure of the Church. Be that as it may, few men have done more to hasten the coming of the Kingdom of God upon earth.